Perspectives on the DIVINE COMEDY

PERSPECTIVES
ON THE
DIVINE
COMEDY

*

Thomas G. Bergin

INDIANA UNIVERSITY PRESS
BLOOMINGTON & LONDON

Copyright © 1967 by Rutgers, The State University
First Midland Book edition 1970 by arrangement with
Rutgers University Press

ALL RIGHTS RESERVED

Library of Congress catalog card number: 66-28134
ISBN: 253-20138-X
Manufactured in the United States of America

For Annette Dobbin
good colleague, good friend

FOREWORD

*

The three essays that compose this book were originally given as the Queens Lectures at Rutgers University in the late autumn of 1965. Aside from the addition of footnotes and a few modifications in phraseology no changes have been made in the text.

I should like to express my thanks to the University for inviting me to participate in an enterprise that I found exciting and pleasant. I am particularly grateful to Professor Remigio Pane and his colleagues for the warmth and cordiality of their reception. And I am appreciative too of the courtesy and patience of a responsive and faithful audience.

THOMAS G. BERGIN

Timothy Dwight College
New Haven

CONTENTS

*
* *
*

Foreword (*vii*)

I

INGREDIENTS AND PROPORTION:
The World of the Comedy
(3)

II

THEMES AND VARIATIONS:
The Design of the Comedy
(37)

III

WHOSE DANTE? WHICH *Comedy?*
(71)

Notes (105)
Index (111)

Perspectives on the DIVINE COMEDY

I
INGREDIENTS
AND PROPORTION:
The World of the Comedy

[*]

IN the opening pages of his exciting and some-- what unorthodox book, *The Fragile Leaves of the Sybil,* T. K. Swing speaks of the "titanic stage" on which Dante has set his drama.[1] If we accept the figure, we may applaud Swing's choice of adjective. "All the world's a stage," says Shakespeare's melancholy mouthpiece, but for Dante the world was not enough. His stage was the cosmos, and the action of his play moves through the three great realms of the universe as he knew it, each seen not only in its metaphysical aspect but in its physical being. A recent critic has very shrewdly pointed out that the general stage directions, the placing of the successive acts, as it were, are given suggestively in the very first canto where the poet, lost in the wood, speaks of the *valley*, the *mountain*, and the *star*.[2] These are shorthand symbols for the great empires our hero is about to visit; lest we think he has lost track of the superficial world of the living, we may recall the "*cammin di nostra vita*," the "road of our life," and "*esta selva selvaggia*," the wood to which that road has led. And the functions of the three realms are summarized by Virgil at the very end of that magnificent and compact canto.

Dante did not create these worlds. He found them waiting for him and took what he found, elaborating as he went along such detail as suited his purpose. Let us look at them as they would seem to a learned man of 1300, as well acquainted with the authorities, classical and modern, as anyone could then hope to be, and remembering that a part of our poet's intent was to pass on to his reader purely scientific information. Imagination may supplement or adorn the three kingdoms, but it does not contradict any known or posited fact about their physical nature.

We may well begin with Paradise. In one sense this is where Dante begins; let us not forget that, if the wayfarer starts his journey with the lowest kingdom, yet he who writes begins his poem after the instruction and illumination he has received in Heaven. Santayana notes that the poem does not really "end"; [3] many readers have observed the cumulative—or is it circular?—nature

(4)

of this monument of unaging intellect, and those of us who over the years, either by the necessities of our vocation or by choice, move from "the love that moves the heaven and the other stars" to "midway upon the journey of our life" are only following the pattern of the poet. And for Paradise—I speak now of the physical heavens—the details were better known than those of the other two worlds, even though the latter two are parts of our own solid earth. This is not so merely because of Christian interest, with its Neoplatonic inheritance, but also because of the simple truth that for the whole lifetime of conscious man the Heavens have been visible and open to study. More readily than in either Hell or Purgatory, in Paradise Dante realizes at once where he is—certainly after the initial shock of launching. He had authorities both scientific and poetic; it's irrelevant that he did not always distinguish between the two. He had, in fact, before his journey took place, even written a celestial guidebook. In the *Convivio*, which is in some respects a kind of first draft of the *Comedy*, whether or not Dante was aware of it, he had spent chapters describing the successive Ptolemaic heavens and the one beyond them added by "the Catholics." [4] He knew all he needed to know of their motions, their cycles and epicycles; he knew their qualities and their deep affinities with the sciences; he knew too a good deal about their "movers." He had to change his mind on one minor point—the relative positions of four of the choirs—but broadly speaking it may be said that the cosmography and administration of Heaven have no surprises for him. Before we leave it, we may remark, however, on a curious contradiction that I think most readers feel. On the one hand Dante goes to some lengths to tell us that the distances are vast and that only the incredible speed of his flight in company with Beatrice allows him to cover them as rapidly as he does. But actually one gets the feeling of—not smallness, perhaps, but a kind of compactness, a surprising absence of a true sensation of the infinite. For example, looking down from the fixed stars, Dante can plainly make out the outlines of Europe; this is calculated to make a modern reader smile a little. Where is that sense of desolate wonder that Leopardi's shepherd feels gazing up at the countless stars and the remote emptiness of space? For Dante as for his contemporaries infinity was a metaphysical rather than a scientific or even perhaps an emotional concept. C. S. Lewis puts this very well; as we look up at the stars today, we are aware of great distances: in place of distance, says Lewis, to grasp the mediaeval feeling, "you must substitute that very special, and far less abstract sort of distance which we call height." "Hence," he continues, "to look out on the night sky with modern eyes is like looking out over a sea that fades away into mist, or looking about one in a trackless forest—trees forever and no horizon. To look up at the towering mediaeval universe is much more like looking at a great building." [5] In my own reading I have never seen the modern attitude better illustrated than it is in MacLeish's sonnet "The End of the World," where, you remember, while all the circus acrobats and specialists were amusing their public, suddenly the top of the big tent blew off and there was "nothing, nothing, nothing, nothing at all." [6] Dante's universe on the other hand contains everything —but nothing.

If our poet could not know Hell in the scientific detail that earlier celestial investigators had made available to him concerning Heaven, yet he could have no doubts as to its situation. English "hell" is cognate to "hole"; the Italian *inferno* and the Hebrew *sheol* have the same basic association of meaning. The Middle Ages, the ancients—including those outside the Graeco-Roman tradition—had all had some concept of the dark realm. We might remark here that even in our own voraciously exploratory century the region under the earth's surface is as yet relatively unknown. We know much more about a million miles *up* than a hundred miles *down*. As for Dante's point of departure, we do not need to look beyond Virgil. It is he who guides our poet to the Gate, and it is a fair assumption that, whatever may be the nature of the denizens, the Hell upon

which that gate opens is, in location at least, the old
Avernus. Dante does not tell us the situation of the
savage wood in which he lost his way; perhaps it is
within a day's walk of the very entrance once used by
Aeneas. Particularly since during the whole descent our
two poets proceed at a very rapid clip; even allowing
for the somewhat smaller measurements of the globe in
Dante's time, it still works out at about 3,200 miles per
day. Dante knew that the Inferno was under the earth's
surface; and from the reports of earlier Christian tourists
he knew it was full of fire, cold, torment, lamentations,
and bad smells. It is possible indeed that some of his
actual furniture is borrowed too, and here not so much
from available classical reminiscences, though perhaps
there are echoes of Sisyphus and Tantalus, as from the
long tradition of visionary quasi-popular literature.
Fracassini cites the Apocalypse of St. Peter as giving
some very interesting parallels.[7] In the Apocalypse, as
in the *Inferno*, the punishments were very specific and
matched with specific sins; blasphemers were hung by
their tongues, adulterous women were suspended by
their hair over bubbling mire, murderers were cast into
snake pits, abortionists were sunk in filth, persecutors
of the righteous were scourged by evil spirits, and so
on.[8] Although the Apocalypse of St. Peter was lost for
years, its influence is apparent in successive visions of
like nature, and probably much of its content passed

into oral tradition. Such visions as those of St. Paul and
Alberic must have been well known to Dante; Becker,[9]
among others, remarks on the similarity of Dante's
Lucifer to the same monster figure in the vision of Tundale. In his choice of guide Dante links the classic and
the apocalyptic: Virgil may well represent Reason or
Imperial Authority or the like, but he is Dante's guide
both because he had reported on the pioneer descent
of Aeneas *and* because he had acquired a reputation for
sorcery, as amply documented by Domenico Comparetti. Even so, he is a strange choice for a poem
in the visionary tradition; the role had been variously
filled by an angel, St. Peter, and Christ himself. Immanuel of Rome, the Jewish contemporary of our poet,
chooses Daniel for his psychopomp.[10] On the other
hand, granted the need of a classical figure, Dante, one
might argue, had no alternative; Virgil, the expert on
matters infernal, and the prophet (albeit unconsciously
such) of the incarnation, was the only acceptable can-
didate. Cicero would not do, and Hell is certainly no
place for Ovid. By the shrewd election of Virgil, poet
and prophet, however, Dante can embark on his syn-
thesis of two very different traditions. It may be noted
that he does the same in his choice of Beatrice, the only
woman ever chosen to be a celestial guide, and so
uniting the apocalyptic and the amatory schools. But
this is to wander a little from our subject.

As for Purgatory, although our poet speaks of its shape and structure with his customary assurance, he does not always have good scientific authority for what he says. Purgatory rests on less firm scriptural authority than its fellow kingdoms; not all Christian denominations accept the doctrine today. Indeed, however sound the basis may be, the early Christians did not show much interest in Purgatory, probably because they thought in terms of an immediate and personal judgment and believed that the world would not have long to wait for the final and general one. As the High Tribunal tended to recede more and more into the indefinite future, interest in the temporary residence of the élite began to grow. The physical situation of the realm was as uncertain as its doctrinal basis was tentative. There was no generally accepted place. If *up* is Heaven and *down* is Hell, there is really only sidewise left. Pope Gregory, who is generally given credit for being the first to promulgate a clear-cut doctrine of Purgatory, seems to suggest by one of his illustrations— a repentant bishop seated in a fiery furnace within a bathing establishment—that it is right here on earth. Bede speaks of purgatorial fires as not very different from Hell fires save that they serve for purification as well as punishment; both burn "in a dark valley." Alberic's Purgatory is a plain, and Tundale gives us alternating high mountains and deep valleys with appropriate embellishments of torture. Inevitably the situation of Purgatory became associated with that of the garden of Eden; Sir Owen of St. Patrick's Purgatory finds himself, after passing through a high wall, in the garden itself. Older legends had spoken of it as being on an island or on a high mountain reaching to the moon.[11] Dante had therefore less certain authority and a wider range of choice in the placing of his mount. Like some of his predecessors he crowns the realm with the Earthly Paradise, adding to it the rivers of classical association. Rüegg finds Old Testament, classical, Christian, and Celtic elements happily combined in the lofty garden.[12] As for putting Purgatory in the antipodes, both poetic and theological reasoning would seem to justify its presence directly opposite Jerusalem; whether it was the voyage of St. Brendan or that of the Genoese Vivaldi brothers in 1291 that opened Dante's mind to a consideration of the previously unexplored and presumably uninhabited sphere of water it is hard to say. We must admire, in any case, I think, the deftness with which he prepares us for finding it there by the anticipatory hint provided by the tale of Ulysses.

He needed the mountain too—instinctively and consciously. We might well have found it there even without the example of his predecessors in the visionary school. If the way of damnation is ever downward,

deeper and deeper into a hole, then the way of salvation must of necessity be the reverse. And so the successive terraces are symbolic requirements to mark the
stages of ascent, even as the successive ledges and pits
are necessary to indicate progressive degradation from
sin to ever more horrible sin.

At the same time the Purgatory dwellers must be
earthbound; if there is to be ascent, as there must be, it
should not be confused with the swift upward flight of
the soul unimpeded either by the stain of sin or its
lingering memory. I have always felt, as to the profile
of Purgatory, that the conventional drawings that show
it as a kind of seven-tiered wedding cake miss the statement of Virgil in Canto IV that, as one goes up, the
ascent becomes easier. I do not think that is meant to be
only allegorical—in fact, I think that in the whole
Comedy allegory very seldom stands alone. I remember
as far back as the *Vita nuova* that Dante and his "first
friend" had agreed that the literal meaning should
always make sense even when the allegory was, as it
were, extracted.

We may consider briefly the shapes of these worlds.
A vast hole, a high mountain, a sphere. These images
are arresting in themselves; they go beyond the historic
traditions whether of fiction or science. One may with
Dorothy Sayers [13] dismiss the notion that they may
have Freudian implications, but assuredly pit, hill, and

magic circle arouse our subconscious response, aside from the obvious symbolism of doom, aspiration, and perfection.

Let us see now what our rational poet does with these ancient and evocative shapes.

Putting aside for a moment their outer semblances, the structures of the successive realms, in terms of the wanderer's experience of them, have much in common. In all cases there is a kind of vestibule or entrance area, a series of functional compartments, and a climactic division. I speak of the worlds here and not the *cantiche*, though the physical and thematic categories are sometimes hard to keep apart. Hell has its well-known vestibule and one might even say that the first circle is somehow a middle ground too. There is correspondingly a sizable antepurgatory—one of Dante's most original and, I think, happiest inventions; giving us, as Wilkins has observed, a period of surcease between two gamuts of pain and torture.[14] In Heaven too the anteroom is there; it is the circle of fire which we pass through with rocket-like velocity, which yet leaves Beatrice time for a tidy little homily before we are landed in the first sphere of the moon. The concurrence in number of the subdivisions is a commonplace of Dante criticism; we shall here merely note that the numbers three, seven, and ten appear in all the kingdoms. Three is the number of the major divisions: In-

continence, Violence, and Fraud in Hell; Love misdirected, insufficient or excessive in Purgatory; in the
Paradise the triad is appropriately less clearly sub-
divided, but there is certainly a difference in the three
lower heavens, marked by one of the few physical in-
dications possible for the poet to call on, the shadow
of the earth, and the six upper spheres, of which the
last trio is given over to recognized saints and angels.
The addition of the vestibule to the Inferno and the
Empyrean to Paradise brings us up to the perfect number. In the case of Purgatory, the basic number seven
is easily apparent (there are seven separate terraces),
and it is possible to find sevens lurking in the construction of the other kingdoms as well, seven strictly plane-
tary heavens, for example; as for building the purgatorial sections up to ten, with a little good will one can
do that too; to me there has always seemed to be a
special little zone between the time that Dante leaves
the Vale of the Princes and actually enters the first
terrace: just room enough for a confessional, shall we
say? All of these divisions are clearly delineated by
moments in the narrative and often by actual physical
barriers: those of Hell, in which rivers, gulches, mon-
sters, and giants play their part, are too well known to
comment on; they are all clearly emphasized; those of
Purgatory are in general somewhat monotonously uni-
form, varied only by the nature of the angelic inter-

vention; yet there is a sharp break between the shore area and the true Purgatory, and the Earthly Paradise is clearly set off. Even in Paradise, nearest of all the realms to being one and indivisible, we have not only, as noted, the reference to the earth's shadow, but also significant stress on the poet's ascent from the heaven of Saturn to that of the fixed stars. The variation of emphasis in the structural elements has its effect on the texture of the *cantiche*. In Hell, for example, not only are the main divisions clearly marked but also the subdivisions, physically so in the successive circles of the violent and the ten *Malebolge*, by clear indication of the poet in the ice pack of Hell's basement. In fact we have no fewer than twenty-four subdivisions packed into thirty-two cantos. Professor De Negri remarks on the isolation of the individual canto in Hell; one can read the *Inferno* canto by canto, he says, and each one contains a "surprise" [15]—in fact, we might add, some contain two. In the *Purgatorio*, on the other hand, although it is possible to see philosophical or theological subdivisions in the antepurgatory, in fact it presents itself to the reader as one rather large area, while at the other end the Earthly Paradise takes up the last six cantos. This gives us only eighteen cantos for the mountain itself, but since there are only seven divisions, the average space for each works out at more than two and a half cantos. Most spacious of all is Paradise, since Dante arrives in the moon at the expense of only one canto, and even if we leave out the last four as belonging to the Empyrean and so another paradise, or a paradise beyond Paradise, we still have twenty-eight cantos for nine physical divisions, or over three each. These arid statistics demonstrate in their fashion why Hell seems so overcrowded and dense and also explain its staccato rhythm and anxious pace; leisure creeps into the Purgatory, where there is time for unhurried conversation, and is abundant in the Paradise, which runs beyond conversation into lengthy lectures.

The differences of landscape are likewise notable. Hell is certainly the most varied; it has rivers, trees, deserts, swamps, lakes (if we may think of the boiling pitch as such), and ice surfaces. It has a number of meteorological features too, rain in the third circle—no one seems ever to have asked where it comes from; a puzzling detail, since there is no sky—fiery flakes, winds, and even, in Limbo, a bit of grass and a brook and, it would seem, fair weather. Purgatory has not quite the same range; it does of course have stars, moon, and sun, and, if we look to the Earthly Paradise, trees, water, and a gentle if persistent breeze. The Vale of the Princes is a pleasant oasis, while at the other extreme the third terrace is a nasty smog belt. In Heaven there is no landscape; only the moon seems to have any texture of its own; light and color must take the place of such physical and meteorological elements as we find in the other kingdoms. The Inferno comes out ahead in the matter of fauna too: it has birds (of a sort), snakes, worms, and insects. We have to look to the Earthly Paradise again before we find any creature other than man; birds sing in the delectable forest of our first ancestors, but otherwise the mount is barren of animal life. I am not quite sure whether the rather ineffectual little snake who troubles but faintly the repose of the princes should count. There are to be sure reeds growing along the shore and two trees on the terrace of the gluttons—hardly excessive vegetation. The heavens likewise are uninhabited—they are indeed even barer than Purgatory since it is made clear that the souls Dante meets do not dwell there but merely manifest themselves to him in their appropriate sphere.

Light and time work on different principles in the three kingdoms too. No sun, no moon, no stars shine in the Inferno; it is actually hard to understand how the poets can find their way. Dante speaks of the fire that russets the walls of Dis, but actually fire is relatively rare in just the region you might expect to find it. We go through the complete province of the incontinent without encountering fire; it is then used to heat the tombs of the heretics, to rain down on the violent against nature, to tickle the soles of the simonists— but these must be rather small flames surely—and to enclose the shades of Guido da Montefeltro, Diomed and Ulysses and their comrades. After this we see no more fire until we reach the summit of Purgatory. This realm, human and close to us in so many ways, is also naturalistic in its lighting; here we have normal illumination; the stars are of course those of the Southern Hemisphere, but otherwise the light by day or by night is as we would find it here. Heaven is naturally all light. It is brighter and clearer perhaps as we go up (though Dante's point here may be more symbolic than literal), but in any event always luminous.

To be sure of time we of this life need the light and motion of the sun and stars, which cannot be seen from the depths of earth. It is one of Virgil's gifts—one of the few aspects of Virgil the sorcerer that survive in Dante's portrayal of him—that he instinctively knows the position of the heavenly bodies. So time is carefully and accurately measured in the *Inferno*; indeed, for the pilgrim poets, the concern with time becomes almost obsessive. Virgil is forever hurrying Dante on; it is hard to understand why, unless perhaps Beatrice has fixed a firm appointment for Easter Sunday. Or perhaps he is simply eager to get out of Hell. Even so, since certain laws are suspended—as noted, the pair of poets race through the earth at a quite impossible speed, nor do they seem in the whole journey to feel the need of food or drink—one would have thought that Dante might have stretched his time measurements too. Perhaps this is an aspect of his moral allegory. The wiser a man is, the more keenly he regrets lost time, as Virgil puts it.[16] In any event, although there is no loitering in Purgatory either, and we shall not soon forget Cato's breaking up the relaxed group on the shore or the picture of the slothful souls racing to make amends for their spiritual lethargy on earth, yet one does have an impression of leisurely lingering in the second realm. Significantly, at one point Dante approves his resting to look back,[17] although Virgil soon urges him on again. In any case time is well and easily measured in the Purgatory even as it is on earth. It is worth noting that as part of the ornament (if the meaning be not deeper) the various hours of the day are specifically described: dawn, noon, twilight, evening are all set before us in detail as realistic as it is seductive. In Paradise time intervals are not stressed; apparently on his way to the Empyrean, Dante spends some thirty hours in transit through the spheres, as against two days in the lower world and three and a half in Purgatory. But the Empyrean—was it a flash of insight or a long sojourn? One might be tempted to think of it as eternity, since the ultimate vision takes us so far beyond the things of this world; however, we do know that our poet came back to tell us of the good he had found, so, presumably, in the literal sense anyway, the heavenly journey had its end.

As for the inhabitants of the three kingdoms a true census is of course impossible. How can we count the weaklings of Hell's vestibule, of which Dante says simply he did not know death had undone so many? And at the other end how can we measure the "flying plenitude" of the angels? But if we stick to figures identifiable and identified, we may risk the assertion that the population is less dense as we go up. I have worked out elsewhere [18] a rough census of such figures and found that the population of Hell, so measured, is 162 as against 77 in Purgatory and 72 in Paradise; this is an even more striking progression if we limit our count to those who have "speaking parts," of which I find some 50 in Hell, 38 in Purgatory and 23 in Heaven —even counting the synthetic eagle as six. Clearly this element too affects the texture of the various kingdoms; not only does the *Inferno* have a smaller line quota for each subdivision, as above noted, but into its narrower confines are forced more than twice as many specimens of articulate and resentful humanity as the *exempla* of the more gentle sort found in the upper kingdoms. And the *voci d'ira* outnumber the *angeliche favelle* by more than two to one. (It is true that the celestials are apt to go on a bit longer in their discourses. The longest

speaking part of any character in the *Inferno* is that of
Ugolino, seventy-two lines, easily outdone by Justinian,
St. Thomas, St. Bernard, and other celestials.)

While we are on the subject of the occupants of the
three worlds, it might be appropriate to notice the
pattern—remarkably consistent—which Dante employs
in dealing with the successive groups. For doctrinal
and moral reasons he is obliged to stress the mass; for
dramatic and poetic purposes he gets his effect by
depiction of characters, individually portrayed. So,
practically from the beginning, in the entire trajectory
of the journey we meet, in each compartment, a multitude, and from this multitude the individual then
emerges. The very first encounters in each of the
realms illustrate this point. From the vast number of
the indifferent, Dante's exploratory eye picks out him
"who for cowardice made the great refusal"; [19] from
the boatload of passengers disembarking on the shore of
the mountain, Casella steps forth; from the tenuous,
hardly recognizable forms of the inconstant, Piccarda
soon emerges with her own individuality. These examples may suffice too to indicate the variations of
emphasis within the pattern, in one case a mere mention, in the others considerable "filling out" of the
individual; the last two also show some variation in
that in the earlier episode it is the character met with
who takes the conversational initiative and in the case

of Piccarda Dante speaks first. But these are only some of the possible variants of the stress and interplay of these two constants. There are even some cases where the mass dominates completely and no individual emerges: the avaricious and prodigal, for example; I cannot recall any division (though I can think of cantos) where the individual dominates and there is no supporting cast. A very common variation occurs when there is a kind of second level of individualization: that is to say, where as against the mass we have one or possibly more individuals with a smaller group reinforcing them, if we may put it that way, against the anonymous chorus. The second circle of Hell offers a very good example of this: a whirlwind of *spiriti tormentati,* a small élite specifically named and identified, and finally the personality of Francesca, which takes over to dominate the scene. So too in the zone of the antepurgatory dedicated to those who have come to a violent end, although the order of presentation is different: a great press of the unnamed souls, a group of the élite, Federico Novello, Orso di Mangona, Pier de la Brosse, etc., and a central group, each given his speaking part, culminating in Bonconte da Montefeltro and Pia. There are a few cases where the herd seems to be missing; the violent of Phlegethon for example; by implication there must be many immersed in the river, but one has the impression that they don't count for

much; likewise, the circles of scholars that surround
Dante in the sun are all filled with specific names and
seem to leave no room for the usual multitudes; here
the mysterious third ring divined rather than seen must
have contained, one assumes, the number needed to fill
up this otherwise scanty sphere. Dante manipulates, too,
the action and timing; the standard pattern is for the
individual to emerge from the mass; that is to say, the
first sight is one of great numbers, and then the vision
sharpens on the figure destined to carry the solo part,
as in the case of Ulysses, Manfred, or Peter Damian.
Whether as unrecognizable sinners in the swamp of
wrath, glowing radiances in the Heaven of Saturn, or
bearing our own semblance albeit moving with the
disciplined docility of sheep on the shores of the mountains, the throng is always present and nearly always
mentioned first, though with varying degrees of stress.
Perhaps there is an occasional exception to this practice, although those that come to mind are somewhat
ambiguous. If Sordello belongs with the princes whom
he joins, he would be an exception; Brunetto Latini
seems to be an exception but, although he has a canto
to himself, he is one of the group first seen in its tri-
partite collective misery in the preceding canto. Although it may be assumed that Hell is more thickly
populated, I believe we are more conscious of the group
and its activities in Purgatory than in the other two

worlds; this may be because the companies here are more disciplined and described as collective units: a boatload of passengers (there is a boatload in the *Inferno* too, but the souls go in *ad una ad una*), a sheeplike throng, a file carrying burdens, a group of wretches huddled against a wall and the like. Many of the penitential groups chant in chorus: who could forget the violently slain reciting the miserere *a verso a verso* or the measured paternoster of the proud or the beautiful twilight hymn sung by the princes in their sheltered valley? The *Paradiso* does not lack dominant personalities; at the same time, as we go up, it is noticeable that both individual and élite blend into symbolic images; in the great Eagle of Justice, multitude, group, and individual are merged.

The narrative divisions, the stages in the journey, parallel the physical construction of the worlds. In this respect both the prologues and epilogues are particularly interesting. Clearly enough, the groups in Hell's vestibule and the souls on the shores of Purgatory, for all the ethical gulf that separates them, have in common the distinction that they are not quite a part of the main kingdom. Their destinies differ: the *ignavi* never will be ready to move on, while by contrast the waiting souls on the hillside are certain to be promoted even if it be only on Judgment Day; this points up the static nature of Hell, its fixed and irrevocable character, as against the feeling of movement, of physical progress that characterizes Purgatory. But in the sense of fringe or frontier colonies the correspondence is plain.

These preliminary zones are paralleled in the *Paradiso* by the circle of fire; granted we cannot in terms of the story find a similar colony of souls, but, as far as the narrator is concerned, the zone fulfills a like function, allowing time for some preliminary instruction on the nature of the heavenly ascent, even as Virgil's talk and the inscription on the gate prepare him for Hell; in the second kingdom the antepurgatory from Cato to Sordello enlarges this area of preparation considerably. But there is also, it seems to me, a phase preliminary even to the vestibule phase. Each world has a kind of jumping-off place—we might almost call it a "staging area"—in the world preceding it. This is most evident in the case of Paradise. Certainly from the time Dante is bathed in Lethe—and I would myself put it back as far as Virgil's words at the end of *Purgatorio* XXVII—we are out of Purgatory proper; Eliot [20] and others have seen the adumbrations if not the beginnings of Paradise in those last cantos. But the correspondence can be found in infernal and purgatorial terms too. The action of the first two cantos of the poem takes place not in Hell but in the living world and yet lays the groundwork for the journey to the land of darkness. So too, I think, once we have turned our backs on

Satan, true Hell is behind us (has not Virgil said, "we have seen everything"?), and the long climb up, accompanied by the murmur of the river of Lethe, is a foretaste of the climb up the mountainside. Again, for reasons in which, no doubt, we could find some doctrinal motivation but which are, I am inclined to think, essentially aesthetic, these preliminary phases are outlined with varying degrees of emphasis—but they are all detectable—and in each realm the journey ends in a spectacular climax. The vision of Lucifer, of Revelation, and ultimately of the Godhead are carefully calculated high notes: Dante is not inclined to bring his worlds to an end with a whimper.

We should remark, I think, that the triad of the supernatural worlds is flanked by two other areas which, strictly speaking, in terms of the poem if not of the cosmos, do not belong to the structure: two handles, one might say, enabling us to raise the beautiful bowl. The earth surface of our hemisphere—which is to say, Dante's own world, to which the first two cantos are dedicated—while it is assuredly a part of the cosmos, is not a part of the scenery of the underworld. It has a nature of its own too, its own special cast of characters, I believe its own rhythm. But it is particularly important as the world of constant reference. Let us bear in mind that if Dante the pilgrim leaves it behind with that line of almost Stoic acceptance of his destiny which concludes Canto II, *Or va, che un sol volere è d'ambedue* ("Lead on, since one sole will now moves us both"),[21] Dante the poet never abandons it. When criticism—I have in mind particularly discussions of the figures in the *Comedy* such as those of Auerbach or Yvonne Batard—speaks of the richness of the life of the *Comedy*, full of cranes, starlings, larks, or containing scenes of farm life, city life, home life, let us remember that none of all this actually appears in the spirit worlds. There are no mice or frogs in Hell, only in the *Inferno*, no sheep graze on the hillside of the mountain although they adorn the *Purgatorio*, and the lark we remember that "soars in the air and then falls silent satiate with the sweetness of its song"[22] is no celestial native, though the *Paradiso* would not be the same without her. Is this but another way of voicing the old truism that Dante takes his own world with him? It is, perhaps, but it is also, to put it in other terms, to say that our geometrist, cosmographer, and ethical philosopher, our mathematical categorizer of space and sin is also a poet.

The other handle of the bowl takes up four cantos only but is more distinctive in a way, being, as our familiar surface is not, completely out of the physical cosmos, or we should say rather that it includes and absorbs the cosmos, at once obliterating it and glorifying it. In the Rose we are beyond the flesh and its crude and pathetic contingencies, its deviations, aspirations and unanswered questions. Here we shall see "bound in love within one volume" [23] all the loose and disconnected pages of our cognitions and intuitions. We cannot say that the memories of that ultimate vision dominate and nourish the wayfarer's account as do the memories of his earthly life, of battles witnessed and shipyards visited and mosquitoes rising to plague him in the summer twilight. Yet in a way it is the presence of that vision, the goal of the wayfarer as it is the starting point of the poet, that guides the hand of the cartographer and directs the thought of the philosopher. Wayfarer and poet are one when the vision ends, leaving its distilled sweetness to abide in the heart; [24] they are likewise one when they hear from Virgil the statement meant even more for Dante than for his mentor: *I' son Beatrice che ti faccio andare* ("I am Beatrice who bid you go").[25]

As the physical worlds portrayed—the cosmos—are the creation of one mind, so the "beautiful fiction" which fills them is the creation of one poet, telling of the experiences of one man, who happens to be himself. The author is the principal unifying agent of the whole poem. But there are other such agents: the language for one thing and *terza rima* for another. These, on the formal level, should suffice for unity, and indeed they do. But here again there are variations, in these cases not of proportion but of quality. Of the three successive manifestations of the pilgrim Dante I shall not here speak; such a topic would take us far and would call for the study of philosophical and confessional elements that would distort the plan of this discourse. Suffice it to say that all critics have commented, each in his own way, on the three phases of the wayfarer; I have elsewhere called him spectator, participant, and pupil as he goes from world to world; let the reference here suffice at least to show that he is not quite the same figure in successive stages of his journey.

On language we may venture a few observations. Obviously the poem is written in mediaeval Italian, and obviously anyone who can read the *Inferno* can also read the *Paradiso*. Yet differences there are. In the matter of vocabulary it is safe to say there are infernal words, purgatorial words, and heavenly words. Let a few of the many available examples suffice to illustrate this statement.

One must of course be a little careful in this area and not simply document the obvious. Insofar as the language is descriptive, there is bound to be considerable difference in vocabulary; it should hardly surprise us if we find *bolgia* only in the *Inferno,* a preponderant number of cases of *salire* "to climb" in the *Purgatorio,* and the largest incidence of *cielo* "heaven" in the *Paradiso.* But Dante's language is not always simply descriptive of what the traveler sees, and in the areas of allusion and reference we can, I think, legitimately draw some conclusions as to his linguistic intent. It has long been remarked that neither *Cristo* nor *Maria* occurs in the *Inferno*; for that matter none of the cases of *Lucifero*, *Satan*, or *diavolo* occurs anywhere else. Of the three words for "happiness," *letizia*, *felicità*, and *ventura*, there is but one case of any of them registered in the *Inferno*, and that one falls from the lips of Beatrice, who is merely visiting. *Letizia* indeed, because of its elegance as well as its significance, is found only in the *Paradiso*. Another example: we may assume that the souls of Purgatory are as naked as those of Hell, but the word *nudo* appears 14 times in the *Inferno* and merely twice in the Kingdom of Penance. The adjective *duro* ("hard"), not always simply descriptive, occurs 19 times in the *Inferno*, 8 times in the *Purgatorio*, and twice in the *Paradiso*; a somewhat similar distribution is evident in the case of the adjective *nero* ("black"), which occurs 14 times in the first *cantica*, twice in the Purgatory and only once in the *Paradiso*. The word *amore*, which is for Dante a philosophical as well as a theological concept, and one would think likely to turn up anywhere in the course of the various discussions and conversations, actually occurs 85 times in Heaven as against a mere 19 in Hell, nine of them being in the canto of Francesca.

All readers of the *Comedy*, under the shock of the scatological terminology of the second *bolgia* or the gruesome references of the ninth, and, on the other hand, mindful of such odd creations as *immiarsi, intuarsi* and *inluiarsi* ("to *me* oneself," "to *you* oneself," "to *him* oneself"), abounding in the *Paradiso*, may feel that Dante made a special effort to give his first and third kingdoms linguistic distinction. This effort is indeed very apparent in the case of Heaven: of the words actually *coined* by Dante, as E. A. Fay pointed out years ago,[26] the great majority are found in the *Paradiso*, where our poet was reaching for "transhumanization." Spitzer has commented on the special character of the vocabulary of the *Inferno*.[27] Yet it remains true that each of the three kingdoms has its own verbal coloring. To take up merely one aspect of this truth: I have made a survey of the words used in only one of the three *cantiche* and I believe some of the results are worth sharing. First of all, the number is impressive; of the 6,700 words listed in our concordance, about 2,600 are used in only one of the *cantiche*: 965 in the *Inferno*, 915 in the *Paradiso*, and 715 in the *Purgatorio* —evidence, I think, of Dante's conscious purpose to individualize the realms. It would of course be idle to pretend that every word so used is specifically infernal or purgatorial or celestial. Still some subtotals are worth noting. Of the nearly five hundred flagrant Latinisms or elegant words (I included a few Provençal and Old French imports), 340 are in the *Paradiso* and only 75 in the *Inferno*. Animals appear 43 times in the *Inferno*, 10 times in the *Purgatorio*, and only 4 times in the *Paradiso*. References to jewels and musical terms on the other hand are more numerous in the *Paradiso*. As might be expected, the Middle Kingdom has less distinction; in fact, the last cantos of the *Purgatorio* seem to fall under the linguistic dominance of the *Paradiso*. I do note—perhaps it is meaningful—that there are a few more diminutives in the *Purgatorio* than elsewhere, some of them very memorable, such as the *pecorelle timidette* ("timid little sheep"), of which Manfred is one, or the *lagrimetta* ("little tear") of Bonconte. Once in a while there is a kind of linguistic enclave; the first two cantos of the *Inferno* have an occasional word that sounds celestial—and for good reason; the vocabulary as well as the tone of the expository Canto XI of the *Inferno* sometimes suggests the *Purgatorio*, and, conversely, old Cacciaguida in his Martian expansiveness lapses into a Florentine frankness that seems to take us back to his less saintly compatriots in the *Inferno*, and the rage of St. Peter carries him to the use of *cloaca*, a Latinism and so linguistically elegant, but denotationally certainly an infernal word. But it is precisely these *stonature*, if such they be, that clarify for us the specific nature of the language of each of the realms.

The manipulation of the rhyme groups shows an interesting development too. It was Fubini,[28] arguing for the genesis of the *terzina* in the syllogism, who pointed out how these triads tend more and more to come in conceptual or semantic clusters as the poem moves on; this is an assertion that any reader of the *Comedy* will accept probably without need of proof; as a matter of curiosity, however, I have checked five cantos of the *Inferno* against five of the *Paradiso*, accepting punctuation as the arbitrary symbol of isolation (though of course it is not necessarily so). However, even by that crude measure, I find that out of 220 *terzine* in the *Inferno*, 154 are isolated by a full stop or its equivalent; as against the same total number, there are only 102 so cut off in the *Paradiso*. As it happens, my test cantos included *Paradiso* vi, where the account of the eagle's triumphs makes for an episodic pattern unusual in the third *cantica*.[29] Had I chosen Canto vii instead, a much more typical *Paradiso* canto from the structural point of view, I should have come out with a mere 92 isolated *terzine* as against the 154 of the *Inferno*. Yvonne Batard finds too that the quality and number of comparisons and metaphors rise and increase as we move from world to world;[30] the texture of the *Paradiso* is rhetorically very rich, its ornament at times approaching the baroque, as for example Dante's "hoping to be excused for what he accuses himself of in order to excuse himself" [31] (a phrase, one would swear out of Calderón) or such worn tricks as *moto a moto e canto a canto colse* ("matching rhythm to rhythm, song to song") [32] or *come nel seguente canto canta* ("as it is chanted in the following canto").[33] The music too is different in each *cantica;* Geoffrey Bickersteth, one of Dante's most sensitive translators, remarks that "In the *Inferno* it is often deliberately harsh; in the *Purgatorio* it takes on an elegiac tone; in the *Paradiso* it is consistently euphonious." [34] I do not wish to get into the discussion of Dante's style but merely to make the point that the three kingdoms, in vocabulary, manner, and rhythm of speech, do have their own individuality. As we have noted in the area of vocabulary, so too in the related matter of style there are inconsistencies; some celestial invectives really belong in the *Inferno,* while Virgil's exposition of Fortune (*Inf.* VII, 73–96), in the dignity of its rhythm no less than the serenity of its subject, would make it appropriate to the *Purgatorio.* But again, as for the individual words, these patches only throw the proper color of their setting into bolder relief.

In this chapter I have been primarily concerned with setting forth the elements of Dante's kingdoms and his disposition of them; I have had no special thesis to argue but have merely wanted to share the delight of contemplating the working out of the great design. I would like, in conclusion, to make two points touching on the nature of that design. First, if we look back at the starting point we shall see that Dante did not invent Heaven, Purgatory, or Hell. They were theological concepts, they were also to a certain extent scientific postulates; they were, well before his time, entities already alive in the minds of scholars and in the fancy of the people. What he does with them is to give them order and beauty. And the search for order is a large part of our poet's motivation. In this too he is a man of his time; the late Middle Ages was in all areas clutching desperately after order; we see it in the great lawyers, such as the famous Accursius, whose son keeps Brunetto company in the seventh circle, or in Dante's own friend Cino da Pistoia, teacher of the great Bartolus; we see it supremely in St. Thomas Aquinas, we see it in the efforts of Frederick II, the founder, in the words of his biographer, Kantorowicz, of the first bureaucratic state. Not for nothing does Dante admire Justinian the codifier. He is a codifier himself; it is his great good fortune and ours that he is also a poet.

And finally, let us not think the less of Dante because he did not invent his worlds. If he could have, he wouldn't have wanted to. He is much more concerned with giving his work authority than with being original. There is plenty of room for originality in the treatment of his *exempla*, in the parenthetical commentary, in the various tactical embellishments. But for the framework of his poem and for the impact he wishes it to have on his readers, he is well content to associate himself with the ancient and impressive visionary tradition, going back in Christian terms to Christ's own harrowing of Hell and traced by the scholars as far back as the third millennium B.C. He would not be troubled, but rather pleased, by the so-called discoveries of scholars relating his journey to the vision of St. Paul, the Gospel of Nicodemus, or the theories of Posidonius.[35] Such findings can only add to the authority of what he has to tell us. Furthermore, aside from his desire to merge, as it were, into the ancient and authoritative current of prophecy and revelation, he is eager also to instruct his readers. So he does not conceal from us that he learned about the heavens from Ptolemy and the angels from Dionysius and got much of his Hell data from Virgil and his ethical principles from Aristotle. Far from it. He wants us to know that his work has scientific authority and he wants us to know what the authority is. For Dante is a scientist and a scrupulous scholar. Even as Chaucer's clerke, "gladly wolde he lerne and gladly teche." The word "learning" in English has two meanings; as a present participle it is the process of studying and observing; as a noun we use it often to signify knowledge or erudition. In both senses of the word Dante shares his learning with us.

II
THEMES
AND VARIATIONS:
The Design of the Comedy

IN the opening lines of *Inferno* XVII Dante's description of the monster Geryon includes the following passage, which might well serve as a description of the *Comedy* itself.

Breast, flanks and back with brilliant arabesques
Were all embroidered, and in vivid hues
Were overlaid gay whorls and cunning knots
So subtly traced no Turk nor Tartar yet
Their like has woven, nor Arachne's skill
Had e'er conceived such richness of design.[1]

If one views the *Comedy* as a work of art, the image of an oriental rug comes very readily to mind. The patterns recur, certain bright threads, creative, rhetorical, or didactic, run through the weaving in ever new combinations, coming together in knots or colorful concentration at various points, forming designs always sufficiently familiar to be reassuring, never without some element of surprise in their composition or tone.

Merely to point out all of these richly embroidered patterns would form an exhaustive and perhaps exhausting commentary on the poem. I shall content myself with some remarks on a few of the more prominent ones.

Let us begin in an area where Dante is himself most gifted; that of characterization. In spite of the subtleties of commentators and exegetes, which have sharpened our appreciation of allegory and the spiritual *sovrasenso*, Dante has attracted readers and will continue to attract them by his creative skill in portrayal of characters. The magnificent *richesse* of allegory and dogma would have remained unexplored (except for the inevitable small group of probing specialists) were it not for the presence of such highly pictorial figures as the grotesque Minos, the seductive Francesca, the grim Ugolino, or the leonine Sordello. And these depictions, lifelike though they be, and having about them the air of spontaneous generation that we associate with Homeric figures, are yet arranged, disposed, manipulated, and one might say given varying degrees of illumination according to the creator's carefully calculated plan.

For purposes of discussion we may divide the characters who throng the narrative of the poem, whose first impact is on the literal level, into two separate groups which I shall call officers and informants. Individuals in either group may of course take on also the function of the other category—and some may be prophets as well. But the division is convenient for our uses here. We shall exclude Dante's major guides, Virgil and Beatrice, as being in a category apart and as of such stature as to demand, each one of them, such extensive treatment as to make it impossible to do them justice and at the same time bring in the less important and less familiar minor figures. By officers I do not mean simply guides, though there are occasionally those who fulfill such a function, but such characters as the guardians of the various circles and terraces and the officiating personages who are not strictly residents of any of the realms but who aid in the administration, as it were.

For these Hell is our best-stocked hunting ground. It is particularly rich in the number and variety of officials for each compartment. Each circle has its specific warden, from Charon, who is the great porter of the whole vast edifice, to the giants who defend the ice

field of the traitors. Monstrous Satan seals the bottom
of the pit, a kind of rear guard in himself; perhaps it is
in keeping with the perversity of evil that we meet the
true motivator and overall president at the end of the
journey. It is interesting to note that while each circle
has its own watchman, the subdivisions do not. I think
we may fairly conclude that the Minotaur is the general superintendent of the seventh circle as he is the
symbol of bestial violence, no matter what may be the
object of that violence. The centaurs confined to the
first ring are not so much guardians of that area as
functionaries with an assigned task to perform. One
might say the same of the Harpies. Geryon suffices for
all of the *Malebolge*, and the rebellious giants make up
one unit to cover the various compartments of the con-
gealed Cocytus-dwellers. Another observation of a general nature may be made here: with the sole exception
of Nimrod, all the guardians are of classical origin.
Agents of such venerable provenience enable Dante to
give his *Inferno*, compounded for the most part of
Christian visionary and folklore elements, a classical
veneer, a patina of culture, one might say. It is true that
many of the classical figures have suffered some loss of
dignity; Minos verges on the burlesque, Cerberus is
rather disgusting, and Plutus is simply silly—but others
come off quite well. Dante—or at least Virgil—treats
the centaurs with respect (Cacus is a renegade, of

course, and so is depicted in a special way), the Furies have a kind of horrid dignity, and the giants for all their doltishness have at least the majesty of size. All of them, with their names suggestive of the great classic tradition and the sacred legends of old, like the retired colonel in Finnegan's bar, serve to lend class to the place.

Virgil's attitude to each—we can hardly speak of Dante's, for he is for the most part in a state of terrified docility—is interesting in its variation. Although he is a little lordly in his response to the challenges of Charon and Minos, he is compelled to give them a formula which smacks of the ritualistic. He is obliged to reason with Phlegyas and the giants, even though in the latter case he does so with tongue in cheek, and for the Furies he is simply not up to the job without celestial aid; he has even to go out of his own tradition to get Dante past the walls of Dis and in among the smoking heretics. For the bribing of Geryon (we do not, as is allegorically proper and dramatically exciting, know the exact arrangements that pass between them) he is obliged to call on Dante's assistance.

If all of the guardians of the *Inferno* have, as Momigliano has said, a kind of concentrated, impatient vitality that makes them appropriate companions of a Farinata or a Ugolino,[2] some of them rise to the level of noteworthy characters in their own right, significant for their action in the drama and for their contribution to

the allegorical-ethical-doctrinal stuff of the *Comedy.*
We shall cite Charon as an example of this outsize type.
He is magnificently described: who can forget the
antico pelo ("aged locks") and the *occhi di bragia*
("eyes of glowing coal")? His voice, both for its vocabulary and its awesome music, is in keeping: *Guai a
voi, anime prave!* ("Woe to you, O souls depraved") [3]
carries a mighty impact, reinforcing on the level of
action the somber proclamation on the gates of Hell.
Charon is, like some of his colleagues, not only a guide
but an informant and a prophet as well. He tells the
souls (and indirectly Dante) of his function, and he
suggests that the frightened wayfarer is taking the
wrong boat, thereby giving us a vital if almost un-
noticed doctrinal lesson. For the poet is here indirectly
expressing the confidence in his salvation proper to a
Christian still fighting in the ranks of the Church Mili-
tant. Anything else would be wrong indeed. Charon's
allusion to the "other bark" is at the same time one of
the many little threads that bind one *cantica* to another.
As to his part in the narrative, one small problem arises
that has tormented scrupulous critics for years—does
he or does he not actually ferry Dante across Acheron?
Mazzoni, among others, seems to think he does,[4] and I
am inclined to agree, for I observe that *first* Charon
says: "This is not your proper vehicle," and *then* Virgil
reminds him that he has no choice but must obey de-

crees issued "where will and power are one." It would seem to me only logical to assume that after that rebuttal our sulky boatman must have carried out the task assigned to him. And if our author prefers to have his wayfarer pass over in a swoon, it is partly to dramatize the entrance into the first circle and partly for the artistic reason that there is another boat ride coming along shortly; to describe two in such brief compass would be unaesthetic. Nor do I see any other way, in the context of the purpose and nature of the poem, that Dante could have crossed. . . . Likewise multifunctional and three dimensional are Minos and one or two others of the guardians, but since "the long way drives us on," let Charon suffice to exemplify the guardian who is also informant, prophet, and personality in his own right.

The guardians in Purgatory are of a very different nature. The angels who preside over the successive terraces are indistinguishable one from the other; in fact none of them, so radiant is their effulgence, is clearly seen by the wayfarer. A shimmering conformity replaces the rugged and clearly individualized band that had performed the same office in the Inferno. Even the operations of entrance are monotonously similar: a flash of glory, a chanted beatitude, and the road is open; there is no longer the rich spectrum of cajolery, bribery, threat, and subterfuge which made the passages

in the *Inferno* so exciting. All of which is appropriate
to a realm inhabited not by the eternally frustrated and
irascible but by the humble, harmonious, and helpful,
characterized not by the isolation of groups into separate cells but by a quiet progress upward of souls of
sheeplike docility, finding no let or hindrance but their
own inner reservations concerning their readiness. The
symbolism is what we would expect, and the guards
too, since they are of necessity supernatural beings
about whom we can know very little, must partake of
the general uniformity. Yet there are some interesting
exceptions. Cato, whose role is a little ambiguous,
is one. Are we to think of him as a guardian of the
antepurgatory only (or perhaps not even that but
merely the shore line, the port area as we might call
it)? I should be inclined to believe that he is rather the
symbolic porter of the whole island or at least that
part of it that extends through the seven terraces to
the banks of Lethe. If we look for textual warrant,
we may find it in Virgil's allusion to "your seven
realms" (*Purg.* II, 53). For surely the free will which
he exemplifies and which provides a justification for
his rather unexpected appearance in Christian territory
is the prerequisite for all who toil their way up the
mountainside. Cato's paganism in this realm is fascinating, quite apart from the fact that he is a suicide; he
is indeed the only pagan on the mount, since Dante

thought the poet Statius had been a convert. If his presence is valuable as stressing the importance of free will,
it is also evidence, I think, that our poet is not eager to
relinquish his contact with the classical tradition. Cato's
very inappropriateness makes him unforgettable, giving
him a shock value that underlines his symbolic role. He
is interesting too as an echo of Charon; or perhaps,
using the scriptural terminology, we can see now that
Charon, in function, was a prefiguring of the incor-
ruptible Roman. For Cato, like Charon, stands at the
entrance to a whole realm, leads Dante over the first
stage of his initiation (there is more ritual on the mountain shore than on Acheronside, as is proper) and serves
also as a vehicle for doctrinal information, reminding
us of that stern law which must forever divide the
saved from the damned. Viewed simply as a character,
he has even more in common with Charon. Do not the
oneste piume recall the afore-cited *antico pelo* of the
old ferryman? Cato's eyes do not glow like fire, but
Dante's awe at his imposing appearance, illuminated by
the four stars of the Southern Cross, comes close to the
terror he had felt for Charon. And one must admit that
temperamentally the two have much in common; they
are both short-tempered, rather choleric types. If Cato
does not say "Woe to you, O souls depraved," he all
but echoes the phrase in his second dramatic and dis-
concerting appearance at the end of Canto II, crying

out to the innocent group intent on Casella's golden song: *"Che è ciò, spiriti lenti?"* ("What does this mean, O sluggard spirits?") [5] Emilio Bigi sees in the dramatic suddenness of the old Roman's first appearance an echo of Farinata,[6] but that, while true enough, seems to me merely a kind of plastic detail. I find rather that Cato looks ahead to Sordello, with his lion-like calm broken by swift emotional response, and also to San Bernardo, surely another manifestation of the recurrent father—or is it grandfather?—image in the *Comedy*. It might also be worth mentioning that Cato is described as a *veglio*, an elegant form of the Italian *vecchio*, meaning "old man," and used only three times in the *Comedy*, twice for Cato and once for the old man of Crete—another figure from antiquity Christianized for allegorical purposes.

At the upper end of the purgatorial scale we encounter another rather exceptional kind of officer. This is Matelda, who comes to meet Dante at the shore of Lethe in the middle of the Terrestrial Paradise. She must be thought of as in some way a guardian of Eden; she also fulfills the office of guide, leading Dante, without his knowing it, toward the holy procession. She is a functionary of the highest importance since it is she who bathes our pilgrim in Lethe and leads him to the fountain of Eunoë. She is also an informant, giving Dante a full-scale lecture, of the sort he is going to get

from Beatrice in Paradise, on the nature of the garden.
As Gmelin has tersely put it, Matelda's allegorical
significance is clear, although one has a number of
choices.[7] she is generally regarded as signifying innocent activity, the state of man before the Fall, and as a
companion to Beatrice—as in the dream Rachel had
been paired with Leah. Indeed, in recent years her
allegorical role has been closely studied; among other
suggestions is the engaging one of Singleton which
would associate her with Astraea, the Saturnian goddess
of Justice, the *virgo* whose return was sung by Virgil.[8]
But Dante almost always builds his characters on flesh-
and-blood beings of his experience or his reading; indeed, I think we may say *always* if we have in mind
characters actually taking part in the narrative. And
the historical Matelda remains a vexing and, I would
say, unsolved problem. The name tempts one to associate her with the great Countess Matilda of Tuscany,
but it would seem odd that a purely political figure
and, furthermore, one connected with the humiliation
of an emperor, should find this ritualistic and theological role thrust upon her. I prefer Scartazzini's suggestion that the historical Matelda was a friend of Beatrice's, a *donna gentile,* as Dante calls her,[9] and to me
the almost inflamed amatory language with which the
poet describes her bearing, with its clear echoes of the
dolce stil nuovo, is a strong argument in favor of this

identification. Such a figure could very properly lead
Dante to Beatrice, and such an identification would
not be out of keeping with any of the allegories suggested. And it would not introduce a harsh and dis-
cordant political allusion into the peace of Eden.

Insofar as Matelda is a guide, she is most noteworthy
as being the first female guide not only on Dante's
journey but in this sort of visionary tradition. Strictly
speaking, it is she who takes over from Virgil, who
wanders along behind Dante as he follows where
Matelda leads, though with the brook running *bruna
bruna* between them. This marks the entrance of
womanhood into the role previously reserved for angels
or saints. (Of course it is Beatrice who develops this
role to the full.) Viewed as a warden, Matelda has had
predecessors if we consider, as I think we should, the
three Furies as a committee of *concierges* at the gates
of Dis.

One more purgatorial guardian calls for especial
notice. This is the *angelo portinaio* who sits at the entrance of the first terrace. He is presumably of the
same breed as the other angels who are assigned to the
various *cornici*, but he is described at greater length
and has more to say. He is a somewhat unusual figure
in that he is almost pure allegory. I say *almost* pure,
for presumably he has his being as one of the heavenly
soldiery, but he is not named, so his personality is

anonymous. He seems clearly enough to symbolize the confessor priest in the sacrament of penance. His prominence is such, however, as to bring up the question previously touched upon regarding the limits of Cato's domain. It can be argued that the emphasis given this angelic doorman would justify our assumption that it is he who is the custodian of the true Purgatory and Cato's writ runs only so far up the mountain. Yet Cato not only symbolized free will but could inculcate, through the figure of the reed, the proper humility and could teach, by his aforementioned tempestuous intervention, the necessity of dedication to the business of atonement. I think I shall leave the resolution of such matters to subtler intellects and merely remark on the distinction accorded this impressive if somewhat bloodless figure.

In the *Paradiso* we are faced with a situation which we can only call unusual in the light of previous experience. The plain fact is that here there are no guardians as such. Dante and Beatrice pass from sphere to sphere with no challenge offered and no passwords spoken. By the absence of such frontier guards we are given to understand that all heaven is one and perhaps also that Paradise is not a matter of physical measurements. Some such reason must have led to the abandonment of these functionaries, for they were certainly available. Do we not know that each of the heavens has its "movers"?

Nothing surely would have been simpler for Dante than to appoint one to greet our pair of astronauts. It must be admitted that their absence does in fact underline the difference between the Upper Kingdom and the two associated with the earth; it matches, one might say, the treatment given the concept of compartmentalization: in Hell the various circles are sharply set off, as we have noted; in Purgatory there is but a stair to climb and, once past the main portal, not so much as a gate to open; in Heaven no barrier at all save space, easily devoured by the soul following the celestial law of spiritual gravity.

Officers, guardians or otherwise, make up a relatively small proportion of the vast number of characters Dante meets in the course of his journey. For lack of a better word I have called the great majority informants. Their function is to give information, either about the nature of their environment or about their own vicissitudes (this applies of course to the most celebrated in this group) or on ethical, philosophical, or historical matters. Perhaps we should note here that the route of information in the first two *cantiche* is not a one-way street; the wayfarer Dante has his own information to offer in return for what he gets; this mutualism is an aspect of the realism of Dante's vision which distinguishes it sharply from the traditional voyages to the other world where the role of the traveler was limited to respectful and reverent listening.

The informant forms the backbone of the narrative of the poem and is the essential element in its human interest. The informants differ widely in their origins, interests, and temperaments, and in the kind of information they offer, indeed even in their willingness or reluctance to inform. One may venture some generalizations. Statistically a sizable number of them are Florentines, which is only natural and makes for easy comprehension on both sides, although there seems to be in fact no grave linguistic barrier in the *Comedy:* Dante understands perfectly well what Capaneus and Ulysses have to say and has no trouble following what must have been a very primitive form of old French on the lips of Hugh Capet. However, he is most at home with Florentines and ever on the lookout for his fellow townsmen. The proportions are interesting: he meets 23 of them in the *Inferno*, 4 in the *Purgatorio* and only 2 in the *Paradiso*. Non-Florentine Italians make up a large category, totaling 78, with 33 in the *Inferno*, 29 in the *Purgatorio* and 16 in the *Paradiso*. Classical figures number 38 and the rest fall into various categories, all small in number: Old Testament characters, church fathers, and assorted saints, the last two groups all in the *Paradiso*.[10]

The Florentine eidolon makes its first manifestation

in the person of Ciacco, a figure not normally accorded much attention, coming as he does after the high tragedy of Francesca. Ciacco is in fact the first exercise in Dante's realistic evocation of fellow townsmen and acquaintances; it is not too much to see in the *mise en scène* and certain linguistic and plastic details of the Ciacco episode the first draft of one kind of favorite and effective artifact. It is Ciacco who first recognizes Dante, and this is a device we shall find our poet employing frequently, notably in the case of Farinata and Forese, but there are others; it is indeed repeated in the great encounter with Cacciaguida. Even the descriptive lines *ratto/ch'ella ci vide passarsi dinanzi*,[11] which may be translated (to bring out the sharp meaning of *ratto*), "suddenly, soon as it [*i.e.*, the soul of Ciacco] saw us pass over," are a foretaste of Farinata's dramatic thrust into the conversation between Dante and his master, and the *riconoscimi, se sai* ("recognize me if you can") [12] has the same aggressive, half-challenging air. Such is Ciacco's sad state that Dante cannot in fact recognize him; he is going to have similar difficulties with Brunetto and Forese. Ciacco's rather artful *bisticcio, Tu fosti prima ch'io disfatto, fatto* ("You were made before I was unmade") [13] contains, incidentally, a word play which Dante is going to use again—much more effectively—in Pia's account: *Siena mi fe'; disfecemi Maremma* ("Siena made me, Maremma undid me").[14] She too takes the initiative in the conversation; like Ciacco, she seems to feel that one name is enough to identify her to Dante, and no doubt it is, but neither of these characters was thinking ahead to the commentators, who have only tentatively filled out Pia's story and have not been able to agree on the identification of Ciacco. Buti tells us that the name can mean "pig,"[15] as well as being a recognized nickname for Jacopo in the Florentine speech, and if it is indeed the Ciacco of *Decameron* IX, 8, we have a tolerably good portrait of him, "the greatest glutton and guzzler that ever was, though otherwise a courteous gentleman and a wit"— so says the saucy Lauretta. It would be pleasing to identify him with the poet Ciacco dell'Anguillaia as some do: among the modern editors, Gmelin thinks that such a hypothesis is *wahrscheinlich*[16] and for Sapegno it is merely conjectural.[17] Ciacco's speech is poetic, I think; witness the afore-cited *bisticcio*, and the easy use of political allegory; even though he lies in the mud, the substance of his remarks is not contemptible. I choose to think of him as a poet—which would incidentally explain his interest in Dante and his eagerness to be recognized by our wandering chronicler. His first *terzina*—after his introductory sally—is authentically poetic, with the figure of the sack of Florence overflowing with envy and the simple

but authentically Dantesque phrase, *la vita serena.* Like
others of the Florentine chain he is not satisfied to be
merely an informant but passes on, with some encour-
agement from Dante, to prophecy, some of it clear
enough, some a little obscure, and all of it couched in
apocalyptic language.

In his double function of informant and prophet, in
the manner of his presentation, in the rhythm of his
conversation with Dante, in the kind and color of his
preoccupation, Ciacco sets a pattern which we see repeated, though with countless variations, in the other
threads of the Florentine skein. The prophetic stance
reappears in Farinata, Brunetto, Forese, and for that
matter in the Tuscan affiliates such as Vanni Fucci and
Sapia. The conversational tone, as between peers, recurs
in most of these cases as also in the exchange with
Belacqua; these are true conversations in which Dante
himself participates, contributing as much as he gets and
sometimes more, as in the case of the three great states-
men who follow close on Brunetto's heels on the burning sand; and I would say also there is a kind of Florentine language, characteristic of these encounters. I do
not mean merely such linguistic echoes as *il dolce lome*
of Cavalcanti, which is already suggested by *il dolce
mondo* of Ciacco or the somewhat more subtle allusion
in the pilgrim's own *La gente nuova e i subiti gua-
dagni* ("The new folk and profits quickly made"),[18]

which pinpoints Ciacco's *Superbia, invidia e avarizia
sono/le tre faville c'hanno i cuori accesi* ("Pride, envy,
avarice; it's these that are/The three brands that have
fired every heart"); [19] I mean rather a kind of unpre-
tentiously aphoristic manner, as exemplified in Brunetto's *lungi fia dal becco l'erba* ("far from the goat
the grass will be,") [20] Belacqua's *O frate, l'andar su che
porta?* ("Brother—to climb up, what does it avail?"),[21]
and even in Paradise—perhaps supremely in Paradise—
in such simple phrases as Cacciaguida's *Non avea case
di famiglia vote* ("there were no houses void of families"): [22] this is the language in which the wayfarer and
perhaps the author too are most at home, and it is the
language we first hear on the lips of Pig-in-the-Mud,
if such be the meaning of *Ciacco.* To do him justice, as
we leave him, he rises above his surroundings; he has
not quite the magnificence of Farinata, but he is able
to forget his miseries for a while and speak—in a frame
of reference even more lofty than that of the heretical
Ghibelline partisan—of the moral ills which are at the
root of the divided city's instability.

Only slightly less intimate are Dante's contacts with
other Italians. Vanni Fucci's appearance in its abrupt-
ness and self-confidence is not unlike the aggressive
self-presentation of the Florentines; on a higher level
something of the true conversational exchange as between equals is apparent in Dante's conversation with

Marco Lombardo, but generally speaking one feels the rapport is not so close. To Ugolino, for example, Dante merely listens without true conversational sharing and, in a way, that is true also of Guido da Montefeltro, Sapia, and Guido del Duca. This is certainly the case with classical figures. It is true that Dante's syncretistic effort, bold and new, has been artistically successful, and the pagans in Hell, for example, are very well assimilated into the world of vernacular naturalism; in this respect we may admire the *tenso* between Master Adam and Sinon the Greek spy as a seal of success in this enterprise, all the more so because it is relatively unobtrusive. But, generally speaking, our pilgrim himself does not engage in true exchange with the classical characters or indeed the great figures of the past; he listens well and notes it down, as Virgil had instructed him. So he listens to Ulysses and Statius and Justinian, for example, and indeed merely looks at such figures as Alexander, Curio, and Manto.

Special threads are woven very cunningly into the general design of characterization. Paralleling the Florentine there is what we might call the Ghibelline; these currents coincide in the figure of Farinata, still obsessed with the fate of his city yet complacent in the knowledge that his eternal residence is also that of the Emperor and the Cardinal; the threads unite again in the supreme figure of Cacciaguida. There is a golden

thread for poets too; if Ciacco be not one, Brunetto
certainly is; Bonagiunta and Guido Guinizelli appear
in Purgatory, and Folquet de Marselha in the Heaven
of Venus serves to combine in the *Comedy,* as he did in
life, the double role of troubadour (with retrospective
linkage to Bertran de Born and Arnaut Daniel) and
ecclesiastic, concerned, with a curious echo of that
pseudo-Franciscan Guido da Montefeltro, with the
lethargy of the papacy in pursuing the noble enterprise
of the crusades. There is a thread of amorous womanhood, too: Francesca, Pia, and Cunizza, all Italians, we
may note, and one of them Tuscan, as is also the gentle
Piccarda. Let us leave the area of characterization with
the observation that there is not a single character in
the *Comedy* (other than those merely mentioned in
categories) that does not send one's memory back or
forward to an affiliate, a kinsman; yet at the same time
there is no case of a character given any semblance of
life at all (and Dante can do it in one line of a catalogue)
who is not distinct and memorable in his own right—
from Jason, who "retains so much of his royal aspect," [23] to Sigier de Brabant, "who on the street of
Straw/Syllogized truths that made him envy's mark." [24]
Since we have alluded to catalogues, let us say a word
about Dante's manipulation of that formidable weapon
of the mediaeval author. This will serve to illustrate
the broad category of recurrent rhetorical tools which

Dante employs with such skill. No writer who aspired to respect among the learned in the Middle Ages would have dared to write a great work without bringing in catalogues; this encyclopedic device gave scope to the writer not only to display his erudition but by arrangement and inclusion or omission to indicate his critical attitudes. As for Dante's catalogues, the first point I would make is that there are many more in the *Comedy* than the reader is likely to be aware of.

They cover a wide area of subjects. There are catalogues of classical personages, Old Testament figures, contemporary princes, and great champions of the faith. There are smaller ones, slipped in as it were, of illustrious lovers, despots of Romagna, celebrated traitors. They range widely in nature, from simple lists of names at the purely encyclopedic end to the other extreme when, with descriptive phrases and insertion of one or more members into the narrative, they hardly seem to be catalogues at all and shade off into simple groups. Canto IV of the *Inferno* contains specimens of both sorts: the somewhat lengthy and purely informational roll call of great figures, largely classical, at the end exemplifies one kind; the little company, although hardly more than the names are given, of ancient poets who welcome Dante to be sixth among them is the other extreme. The larger catalogue in this canto may also serve to illustrate Dante's sense of discretion in this

area; the list is indeed long—the longest in the *Inferno*—
but it does not of course contain the names of all the
great classical figures in Limbo. So Dante wisely breaks
it off and saves the second instalment for the *Purgatorio*, where we hear from Statius of other great figures
detained *fra color che son sospesi* ("among those who
are suspended"). Equally deft is the breaking up of the
Old Testament catalogue; some names are given us in
this same canto on Limbo but they have a supplementary group in the heavenly Rose. Likewise the catalogue of the so-called indolent princes presented by
Sordello is filled out by the indignant enumeration of
unworthy kings in *Paradiso* XIX. I think too the placing of some of the more memorable catalogues calls for
comment; the classical figures both in the *Inferno* and
the *Purgatorio* redress a little the emphasis, of necessity
quite strong, on the great number of figures from the
contemporary world which appear in the narrative or
on the lips of the informants. In similar fashion in the
Paradiso, the leading roles are assigned to great figures
somewhat remote from Dante's world—Justinian, St.
Thomas, and the like—and the very long register of
Florentine family names called out by Cacciaguida
brings in the Florentine sauce which otherwise would
be missed if the mixture is to be consistent. Dante makes
use of his catalogues for dramatic effect too; it is worth
noticing that the final cantos of the poem make very

skillful use of a catalogue—or perhaps two catalogues—
to ornament and give meaning to the Rose; at least
one aspect of the procession on the summit of the Holy
Mount is that of a catalogue, albeit a catalogue in motion; we may argue, if we look for symmetry, that the
trio of sinners in the jaws of Satan makes up a catalogue (and if it is a small one, why so much the better
for humanity) of the really fundamental traitors.

It is in these two general areas, those of the fictional
substance of the work and the rhetorical embellish-
ment, that the poet's artistry, polishing, setting, and
resetting his constants can be more easily seen and best
appreciated. I do not apologize for having spent what
may seem a disproportionate amount of time in these
regions. In truth, there is much left unsaid. In the sector
of the story itself the setting is no less worthy of our
attention than the cast of characters; as a kind of case
study one might have considered, for example, our
poet's treatment of rivers and waterways: we could
have noted how the rivers of Hell are experienced and
differentiated, how the streams of our own earth are
cunningly brought in by reference, to color an episode
or reinforce a descriptive detail or underline a moral
lesson. The torrential Archiano bears off the body of
the violent Bonconte, Manfred's bones lie beside the
Verde, its name suggestive of his well-founded hope, as
the rhyme implies; the remote and cruel Danube and

Don are cited to give us some idea of the horror of Cocytus. To both Tiber and Arno are assigned roles half realistic, half symbolic. And we could say the whole poem is bracketed by the metaphysical rivers of despair and grace, for both of which our poet uses the rather rare term *fiumana*.

So, too, we could have added to our brief analysis of catalogues some discussion of other rhetorical weapons, finding again the same tactical sophistication in recurrence and adaptation. Certain figures have a strong appeal for our poet: it is sufficient to mention bird similes, ship images or bow and arrow symbolism to indicate what I mean. These are the spices of the dish, one might say; we could have commented too on the bitter sauces of irony and invective, or on the humbler but basic linguistic ingredients: alliteration, verbal association, or rhyme itself. But I wish to discuss yet another element and a very important one. If I do not give it its proper allotment of space here, it is, frankly, because the material lends itself better to exploration from another point of view and one more suited to the next chapter.

If we may say that the bones of the *Comedy* are its framework of naturalistic and symbolical backdrops and its blood is provided by the pulsating vitality of the characters, it is equally clear that its spirit is in the manifestation of the author's intellectual interest, doc-

trinal, ethical, political, or literary. The *Comedy* is not
written for art's sake, although it is a work of art; it is
written for the guidance of its readers; the author hopes
that we shall not find it devoid of grace for us. This
does not of course mean that Dante was not concerned
with artistic values. Buxton in his chapter, "Poets or
Prophets?" says that to Dante, as also to Virgil, the
problem of the didactic versus the aesthetic would have
had no meaning whatever; the relative spheres had not
been differentiated.[25] Perhaps this is overstating it a
little; one recalls the passage in the *Convivio* where
Dante affirms that if the substance of a composition is
not easy to digest at least the form should be made as
seductive as possible,[26] which indicates, it would seem,
some distinction in his mind. But in any event it is certainly true that Dante never wrote without purpose,
either pedagogical or homiletic. And the *Comedy* is no
exception.

First and foremost, it is shot through with exposition
of Christian dogma. The whole allegory is one of salvation, and quite aside from that there are patches
given over to unabashed inculcation of the true faith;
some central points recur, such as the aforesaid law
which divides forever the damned from the elect, ini-
tially stated by Beatrice in her discourse reported by
Virgil (*Inf.* ii) and reinforced by Cato's austere statement on the shore of Purgatory. The proportion of

overt instruction grows as we move up from *cantica*
to *cantica*; it becomes so large in the *Paradiso* that many
have found that particular realm rather hard to take:
Quasimodo remarks, paraphrasing Croce, that in the
ultimate kingdom Dante is no longer a pupil of the
Muses but rather of St. Thomas Aquinas,[27] but in a
sense he always had been; it is only that here, having
dispensed with those whose bark is too frail to follow
in his wake, he can afford to throw off the veil (we
may follow Dante, surely, in permitting ourselves an
occasional mixed metaphor) and reveal to us his fundamental purpose.

Allied to religious instruction is the ethical. Dante
was in fact social-minded. Santayana says he talks too
much about himself,[28] but in spite of the confessional
aspect of the *Comedy*, with its very proper element of
Christian egocentricity, our poet is a man of social concerns: he knows that man is meant to be a *cive*, a
part of society. If he is a mystic, he is not of the kind
we normally apply that term to; we find little of the
rapture of St. Juan de la Cruz in him; it is in this sense
that Charles Williams does well to speak of him as
following the Way of Affirmation.[29] Indeed, as Father
Foster has said, Dante's whole notion of sin seems predi-
cated on an ethical-social concept,[30] both as outlined by
Virgil in the eleventh canto of the *Inferno* and as sub-
sequently restated in Christian terminology on the

mountainside. Nor did these concerns find expression in terms merely general and platitudinous. The instability of Florence occasioned by the number of wealthy upstarts and the race for material things, the venality of the clergy, the abdication of the Empire: these special items are carefully enunciated for us in the apostrophe—let us note that here it is Dante the writer who steps out of the action to speak directly— of *Purgatorio* VI. In spite of the passion of the discourse there is a logical progression in Dante's indictment of Italian society and political order: the clergy, the Emperor, even the Godhead are summoned to the bar, and the tirade concludes with an ironic comment on the mismanagement of Florence. These themes are ever recurrent: the indignation with the venality of the clergy is an emotional constant, likely to erupt at any time from the first bitter allusion in the fourth circle through the confession of the repentant Adrian on the terrace of the avaricious up to the scathing invective of St. Peter in Paradise itself.

But Dante has other concerns. His interest in the craft of poetry is overtly expressed many times in the course of the *Comedy*; he is happy to be one of the great six and to have the opportunity to discuss with them matters appropriate to the occasion but irrelevant to the reader (there is here, I think, the suggestion of a kind of élite if not secret cult of the Muses). He prides

himself on challenging Ovid, he welcomes the chance
to explain to Bonagiunta his own poetic theory, and he
rejoices at the opportunity to express his admiration to
Guido Guinizelli and, indirectly, his debt to the old
Provençal school. St. Thomas, like Plato, had relatively
little use for poets and, *qua* poets, would perhaps have
been a little reluctant to let them into Paradise, but
Dante, as we have seen, finds room for Folquet de
Marselha, to whom he accords, indeed, a substantial
number of verses. He is aware of his own poetic ac-
complishment; he points out that he has taken on a
great work and given his utmost to it; he hopes that as
a poet he may someday come back to his native city
and be given the crown. (It is this very crown presumably that Petrarch actually got, being a better manipu-
lator of these matters than Dante was.)

All of these elements that go to make up the very
special thing the *Comedy* is are presented us in ever-
varying combination and, one might say, under different illuminations. A character may be the incarnation
of a concept, as Farinata is of the Ghibelline vigor,
while being still a character; a rhetorical device may be
used to drive home a lesson, as in the celebrated case of
annominatio in the recital of Francesca; an element of
realism may be used to supplement moral characterization, as in that unforgettable scene where the lustful,
seeing the darkening in the flame caused by Dante's

shadow, are first amazed and then, being the kind of people they are, put their wonder aside to talk rationally with him.

The effect of arguments or themes touched on, developed, never quite exhausted, or of portraits first sketched, later filled out, even later, one would say, retouched, is to give the *Comedy* organic fiber and a quotient of the cumulative rare in literature down to our own day. It is true that such writers as Joyce and Faulkner have something of this in them, and we can see much of it in Proust. In Dante it is combined with what I can only call a sense of discipline, which makes it more effective.

One example is of thematic nature. Dante is much concerned with the meaning of love, and he returns often to exploration of the subject. It is graphically illustrated in the case of Francesca, who finds time in the middle of her narrative to offer a few aphoristic statements on the nature of *amore*. It is, of course, love as she knows it, sexual love, romantic love; but the phrasing suggests a wider application. And indeed her statement is echoed by none other than Virgil himself in his courteous colloquy with Statius, but where Francesca had simply asserted, "Love that spares not the loved from loving," [31] Virgil adds the condition, "kindled by virtue." [32] We may note as a kind of rhetorical punctuation that his remarks contain also a *bisticcio*,

love "kindled" "kindles" in return, even as Francesca
had twice repeated the root of *amore* itself. But this is
by no means the end, for elsewhere in the *Purgatorio* in
a moment of very high exposition we have already
learned how basic this rule is; love is indeed an inclina-
tion (*piegare*) of the soul toward that which it finds
pleasing; [33] we have philosophical assurance for what
is in the case of both Francesca and Virgil vis-à-vis
Statius an emotional intuition. But it is also here on the
terrace of sloth, as we see the fee exacted for insufficient love, inadequate response to the highest of all
stimuli, that we learn that love, blameless in itself, can
also be misdirected or even excessive. Finally, in the
Heaven of the fixed stars Dante himself is asked to dis-
close the object and source of his love. It is noteworthy
that he is not asked to define the concept, from which I
think we are safe in assuming that he found Virgil's
earlier explanation adequate. It is true that Virgil's is
a philosophical definition and is not strictly concerned
with the Christian *caritas*, which is what Dante and St.
John have in mind. Yet the definition is not inconsistent; it doesn't need contradiction, merely supplement-
ing. In fact, the old definition, even that of Francesca,
is, I think, latent in Dante's response to the saint when
he says that of necessity the love of God was imprinted
in him, "for the good, soon as 'tis perceived as good,/
Enkindles love and makes it more to live,/The more of

good it can itself include." [34] (Perhaps the word "kindles"—*accende*—twice used by Virgil, is here not repeated simply by accident.) For the rest Dante merely
describes the "bites," as he rather oddly calls them—
collectively we would say the motivation—of his il-
lumined love of God. We may notice that he is grateful
for having been drawn out from the sea of twisted love
and into the right kind. The subject has now been developed from dramatic example to exposition, to yet
deeper knowledge. I do not think anything has been
"recanted" by the way, but merely probed and sup-
plemented. If we look back over the other examples of
love in the *Comedy*, we shall see that Dante is not the
only one who passed from the twisted love to the
straight; both Cunizza and Folquet did the same and by
no means repudiate their past. (Guinizelli, and Arnaut
who goes weeping over his past follies, are in process
of change—and again we ask if it is an accident that we
find them in Canto xxvi of the *Purgatorio*, and it is
in the twenty-sixth of the *Paradiso* that Dante gives his
triumphant reply. How many such "accidents" there
are in the *Comedy*!)

Or another example of accumulation, this time from
the area of characterization. We have remarked on the
number of Florentines Dante meets, the proportion of
prophets among them, and how, occasionally, they
blend with the Ghibelline thread of his fabric. The cen-

tral cantos of the *Paradiso* are taken up by the magnificent figure of Cacciaguida, memorable in his own right
and so sharply painted by his own words and Dante's
attitudes that it is hard to realize we don't actually *see*
him at all, swathed as he is in his glittering effulgence.
But how many figures from early stages on the road
meet in this great character, enriching him and adding
stature to themselves by their connection! The home-
town solidarities of Ciacco and Forese, the prophetic
aspect of Farinata, the paternal solicitude of Brunetto
here come to a focus; even the straightforward language of fellow townsmen is picked up by this noblest
Roman of them all: "And let them scratch wherever is
the itch," [35] "and none/Lay lonely in her bed by fault
of France"; [36] "They, not you, will bear their temples
red." [37] In addition to his Ghibellinism, his Florentin-
ism, his status as a prophet, Cacciaguida has a recognizable aura of the paternal; he is, like Virgil and like
St. Bernard yet to come, a father image. Indeed he is
the father image of the *Comedy*, which doesn't mean
that we haven't had glimpses of it before in Virgil, in
Brunetto, in Guido Guinizelli, and even in austere old
Cato. Observe too the ambient in which we find him,
in the red glow of Mars, rich with Imperial memories, a
part of the great symbolic cross—but the radiant cru-
sader had died under the eagle as well. And as we could
claim for the poem itself, his vision and his wisdom are

rooted in the rugged town by the Arno whose citizens he can still call off lovingly by name; this comrade of Charlemagne and Orlando for all eternity has left his heart among the burghers of old Florence.

Let me conclude, as I began, with a quotation from the *Comedy* itself. As Dante looks up to the serried ranks of saints that line the petal of the Rose, his avid glance moves eagerly about *mo su, mo giù e mo ricirculando* ("now up, now down, now wandering around").[38] An active and thirsty eye, trying to take everything in at once. And this may stand, I think, to characterize the manner of his approach to the countless colorful elements that go into his *Comedy*. We have spoken of the effect of cumulation in his method. We may add here that this dexterous and continuous weaving of the various threads—of characterization, of themes, of rhetoric, of didactic elements—crossing and recrossing in combinations at once familiar and ever new, gives the *Comedy* an aesthetic unity which is in essence dynamic; the whole magnificent artifact, with its separate parts exchanging their splendors even as the stars of heaven, glitters with no static glow, but seems to *spin* before our fascinated eyes.

III
WHOSE DANTE?
Which Comedy?

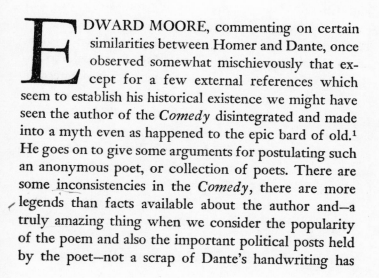

EDWARD MOORE, commenting on certain similarities between Homer and Dante, once observed somewhat mischievously that except for a few external references which seem to establish his historical existence we might have seen the author of the *Comedy* disintegrated and made into a myth even as happened to the epic bard of old.[1] He goes on to give some arguments for postulating such an anonymous poet, or collection of poets. There are some inconsistencies in the *Comedy*, there are more legends than facts available about the author and—a truly amazing thing when we consider the popularity of the poem and also the important political posts held by the poet—not a scrap of Dante's handwriting has been preserved. His name too, "the wing-propelling giver," suggests the mythical. These are all powerful arguments, given good will and what one might call an antipersonal theory of history, to make of him "those poets Dante." Fortunately for the preservation of his identity some records do exist. It must be admitted however that they show us strikingly different phases; if we cannot, happily, think of Dante as "those poets," we must on the evidence think of him as a man of varied gifts and contradictory temperamental currents. Unlike Petrarch, he did not self-consciously reveal his conflicts to the world; indeed, in the excellent phrase of Curtius, he "stylized" his life—or strove to.[2] But even the historical Dante has many facets.

Historical evidence, purely external evidence, gives us a Dante of paradoxes. The soldier of Campaldino develops very naturally into the patriot and statesman listened to attentively by Dino Compagni, sent on delicate missions to San Gimignano and Rome, bold enough and, perhaps more to the point, important enough, to be proscribed by his political enemies. This good citizen and man of conviction is not out of keeping with the docile son, who obediently accepts the bride chosen for him by his father and begets an appropriate number of children. Such a man very properly fills out his career as the counselor of princes, the friend of the Scaligeri and the trusted ambassador of

Guido da Polenta. So far so good. But this honorable
citizen, this family man and political adviser of mag-
nates, has some inconsistent characteristics. The un-
savory Cecco Angiolieri salutes him with gross cama-
raderie as a fellow braggart and scrounger; Cavalcanti
reproaches him for the "vile" tenor of life after the
death of Beatrice; Forese addresses our hero in terms
certainly lacking in respect. The debate with Forese
indeed proves that our Dante was capable in his youth
of coarse jesting with his friends, even of what we can
only call dissipation, to such a degree that he has a real
scare and feels later that he has come very close to the
brink of destruction. His reputation as it lingers on in
the succeeding generation is a little dubious; even in
late life, it is said, he was addicted to the sin of lust and
capable of ungovernable outbursts of partisan passion.
For the latter at least we do not need Boccaccio's
corroboration; the letters to the beleaguered Florentines (not creative works these but historical docu-
ments, written from the heart and with open intent)
are in themselves sufficient indication of the intemperance of which our sagacious counselor was capable.
Nor is this all. This family man, who, it would seem,
felt very keenly the separation from his wife and children and who was later followed into exile by his
devoted daughter, nourishes an idealistic attachment for
another woman, weeps for her passing, and makes of

*

her a lofty symbol and the inspiration of his great work. And let us not be misled by those who would tell us that this was purely a literary convention, imitated from the Provençal, and the common way of life in the Middle Ages. Possibly it may have been so for the barons of Languedoc or the knights of Chrétien de Troyes' upper-class world but hardly so for a member of what was essentially the bourgeoisie. Nor would Dante ever have taken over a purely literary pattern as a way of life without conscious commitment. This statesman, roisterer, and lover, let us add to further confuse the picture, was also by nature a scholar, frequenter of the church schools in his own city, and student at least for a brief time at one of Italy's greatest universities. Truly, as he tells us in his sacred poem, he must have been *trasmutabile* by nature and with eyes always eager for new vistas and new visions.

The evidence of his own works, since we have stepped into this area, confirms the scanty if not inadequate testimony from other sources. It is the statesman, trenchant, rational, and coherent, who advances the three propositions of the *De Monarchia* and defends them with appeals to authority both scriptural and classical and with sturdy common sense as well. Yet the same man has been the idealistic lover of the *Vita nuova*, seeing such heavenly glory in his lady that some critics have found his worship of her to verge on blasphemy. The intemperance, the source no doubt of his period of deviation and dissipation, is evident not only in the hot-blooded philosophical lucubrations of the *Convivio*, wherein he asserts that certain putative arguments of an imagined adversary can be best answered with a dagger thrust: [3] in the great poem itself he confesses to the enjoyment of violence and blood, at least as a spectacle, when he reveals that his eyes were intoxicated by the sight of the grisly heaps of the mutilated in the ninth *bolgia*, and his related delight in low wrangling is disclosed in the next compartment, where he listens with the appreciation of an expert to the exchange of compliments between Sinon and Master Adam. We may note that the somewhat cryptic conversation with Forese in the *Purgatorio* confirms the picture of youthful delinquency, as we should call it today.

Yet this Dante is also a dedicated scholar, at times almost a pedant. The *Vita nuova* is not without this aspect nor is the *De Monarchia*, but the best examples are of course the *Convivio* and the *De Vulgari Eloquentia*. The *Questio de Aqua et de Terra* too would satisfy the requirements for a Ph.D., and all readers of the *Comedy* have noted no doubt with varying reactions that the entrance to Upper Heaven is achieved only through what we must call the passing of the Candidates' Oral Examination.

Is Dante a philosopher? It would not be hard to make out a case for him as such. He certainly thought he was, although in the humbler sense of the word, "a friend of wisdom," as he denominates himself in the *Convivio*. In the *Questio* he goes so far as to describe himself as "among true philosophers the least." Villani applies the term to him,[4] and it was apparently as a philosopher that he was regarded in his own day. To be sure, in the professional sense of the word we must speak with some caution, for Dante did not invent a new system nor did he distinguish himself by any original theories of cognition, eschatology, or the like. He remained, by and large, faithful to St. Thomas. But in the field of politics and ethics, he brings new and acute perceptions to bear. Gilson, in discussing the subtleties of his political theories, accords him "a cardinal position in the history of mediaeval political philosophy." [5] And certainly we must concede that he "plays up" the philosophical chapters of his *Comedy*. Canto XI of the *Inferno* is given over entirely to a discussion of sin—ethics negatively approached, as we might say—and the exposition of Statius on the first movements of the soul and the operations of free will are extensive and brought before us in such a way as to give them climactic importance. The whole *Paradiso* is a discussion of philosophical themes, considered of course from a theological point of view, but the divine science may

be and has been considered merely a branch, though
the loftiest one, of philosophy.

Granting that his major interest in philosophy was
in the politico-ethical field and knowing as we do his
need of *engagement*, it is easy to take the next step and
ask ourselves if our poet, philosophically minded but
too passionate for objectivity, a partisan by nature, cannot be more properly understood as a reformer? Here
too we shall not lack for evidence, particularly if we
note the combination of moral intent, close dialectic,
and appeals to higher justice that combine to give us
the true reformer. If envy, pride, and avarice are at
the root of the world's woes, the answer can be found
by restoring and recognizing the proper civil authorities, and in the context of the times, if we can see no
hope for such rescue, may we not reasonably look to
heavenly intervention? The Highest Jove, who was
crucified on earth, will not always hold his eyes
averted; someday the DUX, the Hound of Heaven,
will be unleashed. Stranger things have happened,
affirms St. Benedict in Paradise (prompted of course
by Dante), even if Henry VII, now secure in his place
in the Rose, was a little premature in his efforts, the
garden of the Empire not being as yet ready to re-
ceive him.

Such considerations lead us away from the philosopher and social scientist alike to contemplation of the

prophet and seer. Is not that the role our Dante truly fancies for himself? He has orders from Beatrice to bear back to the land of the living the illuminating visions he has had in the Terrestrial Paradise, and whether we call Beatrice Theology or Revelation or the poet's private insight into the eternal, we can see in her charge that supernatural assurance that all prophets must have. Equally significant and comforting are the words of Cacciaguida to the effect that the poet's message is good for mankind and, even though some of it may be bitter to the taste, yet in the long run truth will prevail and his own immortality be assured through the validity of his gospel. A respect for this apocalyptic role is symbolized by the presence of Giovacchino da Fiore in Paradise, side by side with St. Bonaventure, no less, as if to suggest that the great Franciscan, who had so heartily disapproved of the Calabrian mystic in his lifetime has now come to be reconciled with him and, tacitly at least, to accept the substance of his cabalistic prophecies. And, as in the case of the true prophets of old, the vision of a better world to come is accompanied by an inflamed and almost undisciplined impatience with things as they are. Dante is a master of invective and some of his most frequently quoted lines are from that inner source of virtuous resentment, often as not put into the mouths of saints and sages: "How many will wallow like pigs in mud," [6] "So that two beasts go under the one cloak," [7] "The evil flower . . . that has transformed the shepherd into wolf." [8]

So many Dantes there are then, both on the evidence of biographers and historians and as disclosed by the revelations of the poet himself! There is yet another problem of identity inherent in the design of the poem: this ambiguity has in fact been in the forefront of a number of recent interpretations of the *Comedy*. For the Dante of his own poem (whatever he may be historically, however he may think of himself outside the work) is not one but two. He is both the actor and the reporter, the pilgrim and the poet who chronicles the pilgrim. This dualism springs of course from the simple fact that the poem is written in the first person. I would like to comment on the fact itself before going on to a discussion of the resultant ambiguities.

Dante's choice of the first person is in itself significant as indicative of the true nature of the *Comedy*. If he took his *bello stilo* from Virgil, he did not assuredly take with it the technique of reciting the deeds of a hero seen from a lofty but remote vantage point. Milton did precisely that, and so did Tasso and, with some difference of manner, Ariosto. The heroic journey as such could be and regularly was sung by someone who had not actually participated in it. But Dante seems deliberately to avoid the third person even in the epi-

NB

sodes of his narrative. One would think, for example, that Virgil could well have sung the song of Ulysses; it would have been in many ways appropriate and would merely have been an expanded version of the brief summaries he gives us of Capaneus, Calcas, Cacus, and a few others. But only once does Dante turn a story over to him to be narrated about a character rather than let the character speak for himself; this is of course the case of Manto. It is the intrusion of the first person into the epic tradition that, in Auerbach's words, "distinguishes the *Divine Comedy* from all previous epic poetry [creating] a new relationship between the poet and his subject matter as well as his reader." [9] Does his predilection for the first person go back to models and, if so, which models? He could have found recent examples in Brunetto Latini or in the *Roman de la Rose*. Both have *exordia* that make us think of the *Comedy*; the *Roman de la Rose*, for example, even gives the narrator's age and mentions his falling asleep, the time of year, and like incidentals. Perhaps Dante is merely following the apocalyptic tradition. Or it is because the poem is to be essentially personal?—and personal in two senses; one because it is to be lyric and instructional and another because it is to be Dante's own story. In this connection it is worth noting that all Dante's minor works are either poetry, *i.e.*, lyric, or downright didactic, with the author in the role of teacher. The *Divine*

Comedy is actually his only work of purely creative fiction. He was used to the first person and probably could have expressed himself in no other way. And, of course, let it be conceded at once that the poem is confessional; the author's name is "registered by necessity." [10] The choice of the first person signifies the decision to tell a story directly and immediately—*i.e.*, as a lyric poem is written—and not in the majestic but remote style of the classical epic. With the election of the first person goes the abandonment of the high style, including something of the incantatory music of Virgil and the grand eloquence which we associate with Milton.

In any event a work written in the first person opens the way to persistent and fascinating ambiguity. For the *I* who writes the work and the *I* who experiences the adventures are clearly the same person and at the same time different persons. On the humblest level of the detective story of what has been called the "had-I-but-known" school, the writer is wiser by the experience of the character written about and so to that extent is a different man. Readers and critics have been aware of this dualism in the Dante of the *Comedy* for a long time, but perhaps our own century has made the most of it, eager as we are nowadays for exciting and preferably baffling ambiguities. Charles Singleton some years ago enlarged on the two Dantes of the *Vita nuova*,[11] and perhaps Rocco Montano has recently pushed the cleavage as far as it will go, seeing in Dante the author of the *Comedy* what seems very close to a repudiation of Dante the character—at least up to the gates of Heaven.[12] Let us now, for greater clarity, refer to the pilgrim as Dante and the writer as Alighieri, and ask ourselves a few questions that will indicate the gravity of this cleavage. Dante, for example, weeps for Francesca—but does Alighieri? Or does he even grieve; does he not rather despise her and rejoice in her damnation? Dante feels a kinship between himself and Ulysses—does Alighieri share that feeling? Dante listens with approval to Nino Visconti's strictures on the faithlessness of women—is this also Alighieri's opinion? The answer is not always simple. Everyone has noted since the poem was first read that for all the sympathy displayed as he hears the tale, it is the poet himself who has put Francesca into Hell, that in spite of Dante's willingness to scorch himself the better to converse with his old master Brunetto, he would have faced no such risk if Alighieri, disclosing a sin known apparently to no one else, had not doomed the venerable scholar to wander forever under the fiery flakes. Must we draw from this the conclusion that the pilgrim sees these dreadful things with compassion only and no sad awareness of the justice illustrated therein? and that conversely Alighieri, the journey done and the vision experienced, no longer is moved by the memories of these unhappy shadows? If Dante listens without demur to such opinions as those voiced by Nino or, more significantly perhaps, Marco Lombardo, who repeats the Ghibelline arguments of the *De Monarchia*, may we simply say that he is after all but another character in the story? It has been argued in fact that we shouldn't hold Alighieri any more responsible for Dante's opinions than we should hold Shakespeare responsible for Iago's. . . .[13] But this is, I think, carrying it a little too far. After all, if Iago had a confidant named Shakespeare, who listened approvingly to his subversive monologues, we might quite reasonably have our suspicions about the author Shakespeare. For our poet is clearly, overtly, and one might say almost aggressively, talking about himself. A younger self, an inexperienced self—but is it a repudiated self? I doubt that anyone will have the last word on this matter, but for my part I cannot feel the repudiation is total. It seems to me that when repudiation is definitely meant to be seen or heard there is a clear signal given. When Dante is too much obsessed by the horrors of the ninth *bolgia*, when he takes too much joy in billingsgate, when he is overly sympathetic to the soothsayers, his deviations are quickly pointed out by Alighieri himself, speaking through Virgil. Or from another point of view, when expressing his delight at the great company that surrounds him in Limbo he says not "I felt exalted" but "I feel exalted," [14] using the *present tense*, it is clearly Alighieri who pens the lines, patently associating himself with Dante. So too in the *bolgia* of the false counselors in the phrase "I grieved then and grieve again now," [15] the link between character and author is made quite clear. Certainly Dante the pilgrim learns much on the way; clearly Alighieri is more mature, more experienced, wiser—better, if you like. But he is different only because he has grown, not because he has changed.

Given such a rich gallery of Dantes, it follows naturally that we have also a wide choice of *Comedies*. One might almost say *quot homines tot poemata*—the *homines* referring to either the writer or the reader of the *Comedy*. The multiplicity of poets and the variety of poems; this is fundamentally of course the same problem seen from two different angles; yet I think the difference is useful to our purpose and that if we shift our focus from the man to the work we shall not be indulging in mere repetition.

The *Comedy* at its simplest level may be considered a historical document. It can be argued that at least a part of Dante's purpose was to set the record straight; it has been noted, for example, how often his account of various matters (chiefly dealing with early Florentine history) parallels Villani. The *Comedy* records many historical events: the beginnings of the Guelph and Ghibelline feud, the disaster of Montaperti and its sequel, the discomfiture of Boniface VIII at Anagni, and other episodes of more or less contemporary history that will come readily to mind. The chronicler's zeal is sometimes apparent in passages where one would least expect it: it is apparent through the invective of Hugh Capet in *Purgatorio* xx, which is a capsule history of the French monarchy, and also in the equally strong indictment of the reigning princes in *Paradiso* xix. In fact, it is worth noting that Empire, Church, and the new power of France all have their historical surveys, as it were, for certainly the account of Justinian is pure history (at least as Dante saw it), and the allegory of the vicissitudes of the Church as viewed by Dante and Beatrice casts a very tenuous veil over historical fact. There is an abridged chronicle of southern Italy—at least as far as military history is concerned—in the gory introduction to *Inferno* xxviii. . . . If we pass to the field of current history, we come close to the essence of the *Comedy* from one point of view at least. Firsthand reports—one is almost tempted to say "flashes"—are given us at frequent intervals covering various areas of Italy, nor are they limited to any one part of the *Comedy:* in Hell Dante himself reports to Guido da Montefeltro on the condition of Romagna, on the second terrace of Purgatory he listens in an approving if somewhat embarrassed silence to Guido del

Duca, eloquent on the Arno Valley, and hears from
Cunizza in the third heaven some rather powerful comments on the low state of morality in the March of
Treviso. At times one seems to reach almost the level
of the café society columnist: no one but Dante knows
that Brunetto Latini was a sodomite, how Francesca
was wooed and won, what was the fate of Pia, and what
became of the body of Bonconte da Montefeltro. The
Comedy also contains precious contemporary insights
into matters other than politics: it is interesting to
hear from a contemporary that Giotto had surpassed
Cimabue, that the Romans had hit upon the system of
one-way traffic, that the Florentines were already
building houses too big for their families.

Yet when we get down to the texture of mediaeval
life, as opposed to the record of events with appropriate commentary, we find the *Comedy* perhaps even
richer. For Dante's world is ever present in his terms
of reference, and his similes particularly are an evocation of the milieu, as we remarked in another connection in the first chapter. Who can forget the arsenal of
Venice, though it isn't in the poem at all, strictly speaking, the tailor threading his needle, the dog rushing out
at the mendicant, the hangers-on crowding around the
winners in a dice game, witches with their mannikins
and potions, shepherds watching their flocks under the
hot sun of noon, the awed mountaineer coming into

the city—the original Little Abner, it may be: all this too is history.

Of a different and even more significant kind of historical substance is the portrayal of the author's own mentality. Man is man under any law and in any age, but there are certain aspects of his psyche which seem to come through as we study the record of the late Middle Ages. Whether it was an age of faith in the orthodox sense may certainly be debated in view of the many battles the Church fought with heresy and even with atheism. But it was certainly an age of conviction; more often than not reason bowed before intuition. For the orthodox—and since Dante was decidedly so, that is the side that concerns us here—it was still true that "Christians were right and pagans were wrong," although under the illumination of Thomism one could use the classical pagans at least as a prop to the true faith. Dante can speak of the great Comment of Averroës, he can admire the Roman inheritance, but in the moment of truth he can only wish that men had stopped at the *quia;* he can see free will ultimately as an article of faith, and his entrance into highest Heaven is granted him not on his knowledge of Aristotle or Virgil but because he gives the passwords laid down by the gospels. . . . So too in the area of politics the mediaeval notion of hierarchy is built into our poet's thinking. He would have reform because the right system is in decay, but he never doubts that it *is* the right system: a great overlord ruling through princes who rule through lesser princes; the *De Monarchia* is the ultimate justification of feudalism—and the fact that it was written by a man who had grown up in what was *de facto* a free city only shows the strength of the political attitude that we think of as characteristically mediaeval.

He is mediaeval too in what I must call, for lack of a better phrase, immediacy or integrity of emotional response. Huizinga puts very well what I have in mind:

"So violent and motley was life [he says], that it bore the mixed smell of blood and of roses. The men of that time always oscillate between the fear of hell and the most naive joy, between cruelty and tenderness, between harsh asceticism and insane attachment to the delights of this world, between hatred and goodness, always running to extremes." [16]

So too Dante. He swoons for Francesca, he all but weeps for the distorted bodies of the soothsayers, he tries to embrace Casella, he would like to embrace Brunetto and Guido Guinizelli. At the same time, as we have noted, he avows himself fascinated by the bloody spectacle of the mangled sowers of discord, he is not in the least moved by the plight of Filippo Argenti, and he kicks helpless traitors in the head with no feeling except satisfaction.

We touch here, I think, in this area of a kind of innocent response, on the element in Dante which Vico
called sublime and on which account he saw him as the
Homer of the second barbarism. As Homer is the voice
of the Greek peoples, so Dante is the voice of the Italians of a similar age when the heroes are so far past as
to become eligible for deification, when reason and
philosophy have not yet so far developed as to estop
the spontaneously creative. Vico, it will be remem-
bered, said that Dante would have been even more
sublime had he known less philosophy.[17] Vico somewhat overstated the position, I think; one does not
necessarily find the *Nibelungenlied* or *Beowulf* any
more sublime than the *Comedy*—though perhaps a case
could be made out for the *Chanson de Roland*. But
the sublimity of a Farinata or a Cacciaguida, I think,
gains as much as it loses by the dimension of the rational which defines them, explains them, and justifies
them. In any event, my central point is that the per-
ception of the universal and hence the potentially
mythical in the contingent is a part of the mediaeval
mind, for which our whole world as we see it is but a
figure of something higher and more permanent. Allied
to this theological concept and perhaps the source of
its vitality was the pervading sense of doom and in-
security. Given the conditions of daily life in the
Middle Ages, such uneasiness was natural enough;

Marc Bloch suggests that it may be traceable to poor
diet, improper sanitation, and hardships of mediaeval
life.[18] Probably none of us would survive a week in the
thirteenth century—certainly not in winter. Dante is
mediaeval in his sense of doom and his conviction that
the world is not as good as it was and likely to get
worse. "So time runs to decay and yesterday was better than to-day," [19] to quote the melancholy aphorism
of Bertran de Born. Dante too saw his Florence crum-
bling into progressively greater evil, the old houses of
Romagna lapsing into decadence or extinction, and the
manners of society becoming more and more corrupt.
The only hope was in Divine Intervention, the Advent
of the Hound, the apocalyptic restoration of the Second
Coming.

To sum up, Dante does not merely depict the Middle
Ages for us, he *is* the Middle Ages, in its ultimate
flowering just before the flower goes to seed. His idea
of progress—this comes out in his political thought—
was not that of evolution but of restoration. He looked
back to a heroic age—even in his apocalyptic moments
he saw the future in terms of old things restored: imperial justice, feudal virtues, and simple habiliments for
the citizens of his home town. And this too is mediaeval.

But is not our historian also an apostle and the
Comedy hence a tract? This can be argued too. "Due
honor to Dante demands that he be admitted as the

leader and inspirer of Christian truth"; so Benedict XV proclaimed in the Dante Encyclical of 1921. We have mentioned this aspect of the *Comedy* in our comment on the recurrent elements in its design; we need not elaborate on it here. Certainly if we are to regard the *Paradiso* as the crown of the work, the part that the other parts are leading to, we should have to concede that the purpose of our poet is the exposition and preaching of sound dogma. For that in the main is the substance of the last *cantica*. The Doctor's oral examination, to which we have alluded, is a kind of symbol drawn from the world of scholarship to underline the high significance of a religious experience. But we do not have to content ourselves with that dramatic event; in the course of the *Paradiso* we have an exposition, all but continuous, of various other areas of theology. The whole cardinal mystery of the incarnation and redemption is set forth in Canto VII. Canto XXIX is a chapter on angelology, and unforgettable indeed is the appearance of Adam (in Canto XXVI), who gives the orthodox explanation of the Fall with a few supplementary details such as the duration of his sojourn in Eden and the language spoken in the dawn of mankind. In fact there are few cantos in the *Paradiso* without doctrinal substance. Was Dante, primarily intent on inculcation of orthodox dogma, only sweetening his preachment with an alluring tale, as in the more self-conscious Counter Reformation Tasso openly avowed he intended to do? This is a perfectly tenable point of view. Particularly if we add that Dante was concerned at least as much with the ethical as the theological aspect of the faith. Does he not tell us he undertakes to recount his dreadful night in the wood (and by implication his whole journey) because of the "good that he found therein"?—nor can we think he means simply Virgil.

Is Dante, being all of these things, yet first and foremost a repentant and saved sinner, now washed in the blood of the Lamb and come back to tell us about his conversion and to point the way to the salvation of others, and is his poem *au fond* a man's confession? This penitent Dante has come in for much attention in recent years when, under the influence of T. S. Eliot, existentialism, and two world wars, the cheerful positivism of the past century has given way to a kind of neo-mediaevalism that is much more penetrating than the innocent flirtations of Walter Scott and Victor Hugo, although it may well be that the seed was in that vast, luxuriant, and somewhat overstocked garden of romanticism. So it is no longer enough for Beatrice to represent Theology (as she did for Pietro di Dante, himself authentically mediaeval, one would think) or Revelation; she must now be Dante's personal symbol of grace, "an image—in some sense of Almighty God

himself," to quote Charles Williams.[20] The limitations
of Virgil, rather than the vastness of his domain (which
is after all larger than Beatrice's in terms of lines and
pages) are stressed, and the study of the *Paradiso,* beginning with the staging area of the summit of the
mount, tends to engage the attention of contemporary
critics. And, indeed, who would deny the validity of
the confessional Dante? I would venture, however,
somewhat timidly to suggest that this does not do away
with the other Dantes. Granted, for purposes of argument, that the story is one of a man, a specific Florentine of a certain age and a certain time, turning away
from sin and working his way to salvation, the essence
of the poem, not only as a work of art but with regard
to the permanent substance of the message, does not lie
in the confession and penance but rather in the nature,
character, and endowments of the confessor. For a
Christian the most important thing is the salvation of
his soul; and this is true whether the Christian be a
scholar, a soldier, or a peasant. But in the terms of art,
which is to say broadly in the area of communication,
these accidents are of the essence. In the domain of
sexual love, if I may illustrate the point by an analogy,
the statements "Me Tarzan; you Jane" and "Shall I
compare thee to a summer's day" bespeak the same
emotion—indeed it is possible that the first reflects
deeper sincerity, greater sublimity, as Vico might call

it; yet the appeal of both the phrases themselves and
the characters that enunciate them is very different. To
have found the "confessional" Dante is not necessarily
to have found the Dante most significant for us; nay, I
would add, not even if Dante himself thought it was.
And surely the richness of the poem, bristling with historical, philosophical, descriptive, and lyric elements,
is sufficient testimony that though the poem may well
be a confession, an *itinerarium mentis in Deum,* it is
certainly a good deal more. What a sinner has to confess need not detain us very long, though we may respect his sincerity and admire his resolution; what a
poet, philosopher, and partisan has to confess is something else again, nor do we care greatly whether it be
a true confession. In fact, if we want an *itinerarium
mentis in Deum* we would do well to stick to St. Bonaventure; viewed as such, the *Comedy* is too cluttered
up with other matters to be successful.

Is the poem basically a Ghibelline manifesto, an assertion of the right of the Empire, with appeal to the tradition of Rome and stress on the secular administration of
the affairs of mankind? Can we regard its central
message as being a rhymed, metrical, and more solemn
presentation of the argument set forth in the *De
Monarchia*? If we cannot, then we shall have to close
our eyes to a lot of things in the *Comedy.* Very specific
indeed is the diagnosis of Marco Lombardo: one sun

has extinguished the other and the sword has been grafted onto the clerical crook. And the eagle of the centurions is given divine warrant in Canto vi of the *Paradiso,* where Justinian, a saint, rehearses its glorious career and recommends respect for it among Dante's contemporaries. Let us note that the eagle, here a symbol of the Empire, reappears in the higher heaven of Jupiter as a figure of justice, containing in the pupil of its eye no less than two representatives from the classical world who had achieved their eminence without the normal educational and sacramental preparation of Christians. For a Christian poem too the number of classical characters is impressive; there are a total of fifty-seven actually present in the narrative and over two hundred more dragged in, as it were, by reference. Dante's guide for two-thirds of the journey is Virgil, representing, we may be sure, not only reason, but the classical tradition in all its aspects, not excluding that of Ghibellinism. If we were to leave the classical element out of the *Comedy,* we should in cold fact have no poem left. Even the chariot of the Church in the symbolic procession in Eden is compared to the chariot of Augustus, and we have noted that it was great Jove who was crucified on earth.

We have the right to ask too: Why may we not simply consider the *Comedy* as a poem? As far as the elements that make it up are concerned—polemical, didactical, philosophical or what you will—they could all have been put into prose; indeed, one may say they all were, for the *Comedy* contains, broadly speaking, everything we find in the *De Monarchia* and the *Convivio*, and the substance of the *De Vulgari* is adumbrated, while its real significance is made manifest in the very choice of the vernacular for the poem. Why *did* Dante in fact turn to verse, one is sometimes tempted to ask. Partly, as he states in the *Convivio*, as a pedagogical device; if the matter is not easy to take in, then it can be made palatable by beauty of ornament. But perhaps it is a poem because our author remembers the promise he made in his youth to create for Beatrice something never yet written for any woman, and for the beloved only a poem is suitable. But if a poem, what kind of a poem? May we see it as an exciting narrative, swift paced, full of things "new and strange" (Dante's own formula as expressed in the *Convivio*), which things would include thrilling incidents, dramatic characters, cunningly arranged climaxes? I believe we may read it so today if we choose. Many have in the past, and even Eliot tells us we need not worry too much about the allegory—at first, anyway. Or is it rather a great lyric? Leopardi so defined it, pointing out that the author and his emotions are always before us.[21] Recently a Russian critic has spoken of it as "one single unified and indivisible stanza." [22] I think it would not be unfair to regard the *Comedy* as a gigantic *canzone,* or ode, observing the basic rule of three in the matter of division that is as old as the Provençal, filling each great stanza with erudition as well as beauty, as Dante had learned from Guido Guinizelli, having always in mind the dedication to his lady, who is—so she says in Canto II of the *Inferno*—the mover of it all, and who dominates the ultimately significant third stanza. I think the well-known repetition of the word *stelle* at the end of each *cantica* is calculated to give us the idea of unity and common direction among the three divisions.

But in fact, though perhaps the tavern keepers who quoted the poem in Petrarch's day (much to his misplaced contempt) may have been satisfied with the literal, most of us cannot be. At least as soon as the gay-pelted beast appears we know there is more in the story than meets the eye. We do not have to be scholars steeped in the mediaeval conventions to know allegory when we see it. The story captures us; the intuition of deeper meaning behind the veil holds us, fascinates us, may even make *Dantisti* of us.

Allegory, then. But this facet cannot so easily be isolated and pigeonholed.

There are in fact many allegories. If the letter to Can Grande is authentic—or for that matter even if it isn't —we may regard the main allegory as being a picture of the various spiritual states of living man as portrayed through the fiction of the journey through the world of the dead. This is indeed Dante's own special kind of allegory, and critics have for centuries now been loud and articulate in its praise. It is this allegory that in terms of the narrative gives us the living character with the implied symbolism built in—as distinguished from the traditional mediaeval practice of giving bodies and voices to abstract qualities. And so instead of seeing a *papier-mâché* figure labeled "lust" or another one labeled "violence-against-nature," we see Francesca and Brunetto Latini and the like. The lesson draws strength from naturalistic illustration. But as a matter of fact Dante does not entirely abandon the old-fashioned conventional ideographs. Symbols surely, as well as actors, are Cerberus, Plutus, the Minotaur, and a few others of Hell's nonhuman menagerie. And most significantly of all, it seems to me, in his ultimate visions, which form the respective climaxes to each of the *cantiche*, Dante puts aside his humanistic allegory and gives us pure abstractions. Satan is no engaging and affable Mephistopheles but a mathematically contrived design of evil. In the famous procession on the summit of Purgatory there is again a reversion to the conventional allegory— at some cost, I have always thought, to the realistic appeal of the apocalyptic moment, with a double-natured monster playing the role of Christ and a three-eyed nymph, hardly very appealing sensually, cast as one of the cardinal virtues. To be sure, Beatrice is there to humanize the episode—as much as any admiral striding his quarterdeck can humanize anything—but with her appearance we are already back in another kind of allegory. Clearly, too, the image of the God-head in the final vision of the *Paradiso* is drawn—perhaps there is no way out of this—from the same materials. And *à propos* of these ultimate visions, though they are a break from the kind of allegory that has given the poem six and a half centuries of vitality, they are certainly an evidence of Dante's discretion. Neither Satan nor God nor the Virgin Mary has a word to say; [23] what a contrast to Milton with his eloquent and appealing Devil and his complacent God, willing and eager to justify Himself in terms that sound to the unprejudiced reader all but intolerably pompous! It is true that in his use of mediators Dante is mediaeval and Catholic while Milton's face-to-face encounters spring from a different outlook, but I am not sure Dante is responding so much to the style of his times as to his innate sense of artistic tact. If Evil were to speak it must of necessity speak with some charm—but Dante lets the seductive appeal of wrong come out in his own allegory through the lips of Francesca or Ulysses and leaves Satan in terrible and menacing silence. And in truth, perhaps Good should never speak at all; it should need no pleading; insofar as it does plead its case, it is bound to seem self-righteous. But I am afraid I have digressed.

The allegory of Canto 1 stands apart too. It is certainly not a part of the main allegory, wherein the world of the dead is a clue to the world of the living, for we are not yet in the world of the dead. Nor is it quite as susceptible of exegetical interpretation as the figure of Satan or the gryphon-led procession. It is a much more personal allegory on the one hand; on the other, it has clearly political overtones. The ambiguities of the beasts, still a lively subject of debate among critics, are teasing, and it is not easy to be sure of the poet's intention with respect to these multivalent creatures. Are they the traditional symbols of Lust, Pride, and Avarice? Are they a kind of literary figure displaying in advance the three divisions of the Inferno: Incontinence, Violence, and Fraud? And if so, with apologies to the lion, who seems a pretty straightforward kind of beast, which is which? Recently I have been all but persuaded by Fasani, who makes the point that what we have here is something at once mystic and Jungian; [24] the inner awakening of the soul toward aspiration is always accompanied by a counteraction of the animal that lies buried in our being, and this animal may be portrayed in various ways as the impediments of the flesh are varied in nature. I say *almost* persuaded, for then I remember that the unhappy end predicted for the she-wolf will have as its by-product the well-being of humble Italy, and if this is not a political allegory, Dante has willfully deceived his readers. I do believe, of course, that the substance of the first canto taken as a whole is an allegory of the journey, of the poet's state of mind and conscience and of his literary attitude and purpose.

There are other specialized meanings embedded, as it were, in the mortar of the main allegory. The action of *Purgatorio* IX, for example, whatever else it may be, is clearly symbolic of the sacrament of confession. Later on we have, following the great procession and after Dante has been forgiven by Beatrice, a vision displaying in quite conventional symbolism the birth, triumph, persecution, corruption, and rape of the Church. The *Purgatorio* is indeed rich in these tangential allegories; another, which is acceptable only if we step entirely out of the framework of the tale, is the abortive raid of the snake among the dozing princes on the hillside of the mount; and of course each of Dante's three dreams is a special vision standing apart from the main thread of the narrative, although he makes skillful use of them in the development of the action. The first one serves the purpose of getting him up the apparently unscalable upper rise of the foothills (and structurally serves to remind us that Lucia is not to be overlooked

in the machinery of redemption); the other two underline doctrinal points that are or will be woven into the
story. Another special allegory is the very vexing one
of the cord tossed into the gulf of Lower Hell to en-
snare—or entice—Geryon. Curiously enough, although
the *Paradiso* abounds in symbolism, it contains little of
this kind of subsidiary allegory, which one might call
anecdotal. In this final world, which is all vision, Dante
has no parenthetical visions—at least until we shift
gears and move into the Empyrean. The varying colors
of the heavens, the figures which adorn them—cross,
eagle, ladder, and so on—are simply the landscape of
Paradise corresponding in function to sand, fire, ice,
and the like in Hell; of necessity, these are symbols and,
given their nature, more clearly if not more truly so
than the rugged features of Hell, but all within the
framework of the main allegory.

However, the point I wish to make is that there is a
great range of figural matter in the poem, running from
conventional, and, one might say, Byzantine abstractions, to the kind of humanistic symbolism which a
sensitive and ethically oriented author might use today.
Dante would have no trouble understanding Faulkner's
Snopeses or Sartorises, and I am sure he would have
reveled in "The Bear." Deeper than moral allegory are
the ancient folk intuitions in which the *Comedy*
abounds; it is, as Northrop Frye has pointed out,[25] in

structure "the marvellous journey," it is the search for the Sleeping Beauty, the Quest of the Fleece—or the Grail. It contains father and mother images, and it has certain archetypal elements of terror, sanctuary, and rapture, the Dark Forest, so well explored by Vico, the ancient rivers with all their implications of dangerous and forbidden frontiers, the eternal fire, and, on the other hand and recurrently, the garden, the consoling stars, the reassuring light.

A word in conclusion. The pattern of what I have had to say follows, I think, the successive stages of appreciation through which readers of the *Comedy* pass. First we are fascinated and perhaps even awed by the boldness of the poet's conception; then we pass on to admiration of the skill with which he manipulates the elements of his material; finally, marvelous as it is, the great work yields in interest to our contemplation of its creator. For all works of art are in some sense *autoritratti*, and the greater the work the more exciting the portrait. Behind the work is the artist, and the artist is the man. "To penetrate deeply into the *Comedy*," says a French critic, "one would have to be a historian, naturalist, astronomer, geographer, philologist, jurist, musician and . . . from time to time psychoanalyst. It would be well to be a poet too." [26] I would subscribe to that, but I would think the first requirement is simpler and perhaps all-inclusive: one must be first of all a *man* and prepared to see, behind both the erudition and the magic of the *Comedy*, another man, gifted in all those specialized ways but gifted most of all in his essential and articulate humanity. Dante lives on— and will live—not because he tells us about Guelphs and Ghibellines or Thomistic philosophy or not even because his rhetoric is cunning and his characterizations memorable; he lives because his poem discloses to us a fellow man, greater in intellectual range, deeper in strength of passion perhaps than most of us, and certainly more articulate, but for all that our kinsman— and, with the aforesaid gifts, fit, as no other in our span of memory, to be our spokesman.

NOTES

CHAPTER I

1. *The Fragile Leaves of the Sybil*, Westminster, Md., 1962, p. 3.
2. Remo Fasani, *Il poema sacro*, Florence, 1964, p. 2.
3. See "Dante" in *Three Philosophical Poets*, Anchor ed., Garden City, N.Y., n.d., p. 121.
4. *Convivio* II, 3–4.
5. *The Discarded Image*, New York, 1964, p. 99.
6. In *Poems: 1924–1933*, Boston, 1933.
7. *La concezione religiosa del Purgatorio in Dante e prima di Dante*, Florence, 1931, pp. 18 ff.
8. See Ernest J. Becker, *A Contribution to the Comparative Study of the Medieval Visions of Heaven and Hell*, Baltimore, 1899, pp. 29–41.
9. *Ibid.*, p. 85.
10. On such matters see Becker; also A. Rüegg, *Die Jenseitsvorstellung vor Dante*, Cologne, 1945, Vol. I.

Notes

*

11. See M. W. Bloomfield, *The Seven Deadly Sins*, Lansing, Mich., 1952, p. 315, note 98.

12. *Die Jenseitsvorstellung*, II, 156.

13. "Dante's Imagery—II Pictorial" in *Introductory Papers on Dante*, New York, 1954, p. 41.

14. *A History of Italian Literature*, Cambridge, Mass., 1954, p. 65.

15. Enrico De Negri, "Tema e iconografia del Purgatorio," *Romanic Review* XLIX (April 1958), 81.

16. *Purg.* III, 78.

17. *Ibid.*, IV, 54.

18. "On the *Personae* of the *Comedy*," *Italica* XLII (1965), 1–7

19. *Inf.* III, 60.

20. "Dante," in *Selected Essays*, New York, 1950, p. 217.

21. *Inf.* II, 139.

22. *Par.* XX, 73–75.

23. *Ibid.*, XXXIII, 86.

24. *Ibid.*, 62–63.

25. *Inf.* II, 70.

26. In his *Concordance of the Divina Commedia*, Cambridge, Mass., 1888, pp. v–vi. Subsequent *Concordance* references in text are to that of The Dante Society, Cambridge, Mass., 1965.

27. See "Speech and Language in *Inferno* XIII," *Italica* XIX (1942), 81–104.

28. See "Il metro della 'Divina Commedia'" in *Metrica e poesia*, Milan, 1962, pp. 185–221.

29. It is true that Giuseppe Lisio in his *L'arte del periodo nelle opere volgari di Dante Alighieri e del secolo XIII* (Bologna, 1902) suggests a different finding; yet he too comments on the greater number of cases of verses ending with the sentence in the *Inferno* as compared to the incidence in the other two *cantiche*.

30. See her *Dante, Minerve et Apollon*, Paris, 1952.

31. *Par.* XIV, 136–37.

32. *Ibid.*, XII, 6.

33. *Ibid.*, v, 139.
34. In the Introduction to his translation of the *Comedy*, Cambridge, Mass., 1965.
35. See Bloomfield, *op. cit.*, p. 311, note 61.

CHAPTER II

1. *Inf.* xvii, 13–18.
2. See gloss on *Inf.* iii, 82–120, in his edition of the *Inf.*, Florence, 1948.
3. *Inf.* iii, 84.
4. In his *Lettura* on this canto in *Almae Luces Malae Cruces*, Bologna, 1941.
5. *Purg.* ii, 120.
6. *Letture dantesche*, a cura di Giovanni Getto, Florence, 1962.
7. In his *Kommentar* to the *Divine Comedy*, Stuttgart, 1955, ii, 440.
8. See *Journey to Beatrice*, Cambridge, Mass., 1958, chap. xi
9. In his comment on *Purg.* xxviii, 34–84. I quote from the ed. of 1896, Milan.
10. See T. G. Bergin, "On the *Personae* of the *Comedy*," *Italica* xlii, 1 (1965), 1–7.
11. *Inf.* vi, 38–39.
12. *Ibid.*, 41.
13. *Ibid.*, 42.
14. *Purg.* v, 134.
15. See Scartazzini, ed. cit., gloss on *Inf.* vi, 52.
16. *Kommentar*, i, 127.
17. *Inf.*, Florence, 1955, note on *Inf.* vi, 52.
18. *Inf.* xvi, 73.
19. *Ibid.*, vi, 74–75.
20. *Ibid.*, xv, 72.
21. *Purg.* iv, 127.
22. *Par.* xv, 106.

23. *Inf.* XVIII, 85.
24. *Par.* X, 137–38.
25. C. R. Buxton, *Prophets of Heaven and Hell*, New York, 1945, p. 11.
26. *Convivio* II, 11.
27. In *The Poet and the Politician* (Eng. trans.), Carbondale, Ill., 1964, p. 78.
28. *Three Philosophical Poets*, Anchor ed., Garden City, N.Y., n.d., p. 119.
29. *The Figure of Beatrice*, London, 1943, pp. 7–16.
30. "The Theology of the *Inferno*," in *God's Tree*, London, 1957.
31. *Inf.* V, 103.
32. *Purg.* XXII, 11.
33. *Ibid.*, XVIII, 26.
34. *Par.* XXVI, 28–30.
35. *Ibid.*, XVII, 129.
36. *Ibid.*, XV, 120.
37. *Ibid.*, XVII, 66.
38. *Ibid.*, XXXI, 48.

CHAPTER III

1. Edward Moore, *Dante and His Early Biographers*, London, 1890, pp. 119–23.
2. *European Literature and the Latin Middle Ages*, trans. W. R. Trask, New York, 1953, p. 360.
3. *Convivio* IV, 14; pp. 300 f. of the Temple Classics ed., London, 1903.
4. *Chronicles*, Book IX, chap. 136; p. 449 of the Selfe-Wicksteed trans., Westminster, 1897.
5. *Dante the Philosopher*, trans. David Moore, New York, 1949, p. 211.

Notes

*

6. *Inf.* VIII, 50.

7. *Par.* IX, 130–32.

8. *Ibid.*, XXI, 134.

9. *Literary Language and Its Public in Late Latin Antiquity and in the Middle Ages,* trans. Ralph Manheim, New York, 1965, p. 233.

10. *Purg.* XXX, 63.

11. *An Essay on the Vita nuova,* Cambridge, Mass., 1949.

12. *Storia della poesia di Dante,* Naples, 1962–63, Vol. II.

13. *Ibid.*, I, 375.

14. *Inf.* IV, 120.

15. *Ibid.*, XXVI, 19–20.

16. *The Waning of the Middle Ages,* quoted from the Anchor ed., Garden City, N.Y., 1954, p. 27.

17. *Scienza nuova prima,* cap. 314.

18. *Feudal Society,* Chicago, 1961, pp. 72 ff.

19. In his *planh* for the Young King; see A. Stimming, *Bertran von Born,* Halle, 1913, p. 27, l. 28.

20. *The Figure of Beatrice,* p. 8.

21. *Zibaldone,* a cura di Francesco Flora, Milan, 1937, II, 1230.

22. Osip Mandelstam, "Talking about Dante," in *Books Abroad,* May 1965, p. 31.

23. To be sure, the Virgin is quoted by Virgil, quoting Beatrice, in *Inf.* II, 98–99, and her intercessory glance is recorded in *Par.* XXXIII, 43–45. But these references do not invalidate our observation.

24. *Il poema sacro,* pp. 103 ff.

25. *Anatomy of Criticism,* Princeton, 1957, p. 57.

26. Yvonne Batard, *op. cit.,* p. 17.

INDEX
OF PROPER NAMES

Contains names of authors and titles referred to in the text; also names of historical figures or fictional characters. Does not include place names, titles cited only in the notes, or such recurrent items as Dante, *Comedy*, *Inferno*, etc.

Accursius, 35
Adam, 91
Adam, Master, 56, 75
Adrian, 64
Aeneas, 8, 9
Alberic, 9, 10
Alexander the great, 56
Angiolieri, Cecco, 73
Apocalypse of St. Peter, 8
Arachne, 37
Argenti, Filippo, 88
Ariosto, 79
Aristotle, 36, 87
Arnaut Daniel, 57, 68
Astraea, 47
Auerbach, Erich, 27, 80
Averroës, 87

Bartolus, 35
Batard, Yvonne, 27, 33
"Bear, The," 102
Beatrice, 9, 18, 28, 39, 47–49, 62, 73, 78, 92, 93, 96, 99, 102
Becker, Ernest J., 9
Bede, 10
Belacqua, 54, 55
Benedict of Nursia, St., 77
Benedict XV, Pope, 91
Beowulf, 89
Bernard of Clairvaux, St., 21, 46, 69
Bertran de Born, 57, 90
Bickersteth, Geoffrey, 34
Bigi, Emilio, 46

Bloch, Marc, 90
Bonagiunta da Lucca, 57, 65
Bonaventure, St., 78, 94
Bonconte da Montefeltro, 22, 32, 60, 86
Boniface VIII, Pope, 85
Brendan, St., 11
Brunetto Latini: see Latini, Brunetto
Buti, Francesca da, 53
Buxton, C. R., 62

Cacciaguida, 32, 52, 55, 56, 59, 69, 78, 89
Cacus, 40, 80
Calcas, 80
Calderón, 34
Can Grande della Scala, 97
Capaneus, 51, 80
Capet, Hugh, 51, 85
Cardinal, the, 56
Casella, 21, 46, 88
Cato, 19, 25, 44–46, 49, 62, 69
Cavalcanti, 54, 73
centaurs, 40
Cerberus, 40, 98
Chanson de Roland, 14
Charlemagne, 70
Charon, 39, 41–43, 45
Chaucer, 36
Chrétien de Troyes, 74

Christ, 9, 36
Ciacco, 52–55, 57, 69
Ciacco dell'Anguillaia, 53
Cicero, 9
Cimabue, 86
Cino da Pistoia, 35
Compagni, Dino, 72
Comparetti, Domenico, 9
Convivio, 5, 62, 75, 96
Crete, Old Man of, 46
Croce, Benedetto, 63
Cunizza, 57, 68, 86
Curio, 56
Curtius, E. R., 72

Daniel, 9
Daniel, Arnaut, 57, 68
Decameron, 53
De Monarchia, 74, 75, 83, 88, 93, 94, 96
De Negri, Enrico, 15
De Vulgari Eloquentia, 75
Diomed, 18
Dionysius, 36
Donati, Forese, 52, 54, 69, 73, 75

Eliot, T. S., 25, 92, 96
Emperor, the: see Frederick II
"End of the World, The," 7

Farinata, 41, 46, 52, 54–56, 65, 69, 89

Fasani, Remo, 99

Faulkner, William, 66, 102

Fay, E. A., 31

Folquet de Marselha, 57, 65, 68

Foster, Kenelm, 63

Fracassini, Umberto, 8

Fragile Leaves of the Sybil, The, 3

Francesca, 22, 30, 38, 52, 57, 65–67, 82, 86, 88, 89, 98

Frederick II, Holy Roman emperor, 35, 56

Frye, Northrop, 102

Fucci, Vanni, 54, 55

Fubini, Mario, 33

Furies, the, 41, 48

Geryon, 37, 40, 41, 102

Gilson, Étienne, 76

Giotto, 86

Giovacchino da Fiore, 78

Gmelin, Hermann, 47, 53

Gregory the Great, Pope, 10

Guido da Montefeltro, 18, 56, 57, 85

Guido da Polenta, 73

Guido del Duca, 56, 85, 86

Guinizelli, Guido, 65, 68, 69, 88, 97

Harpies, the, 40

Henry VII, Holy Roman emperor, 77

Homer, 71, 89

Hugo, Victor, 92

Huizinga, Johan, 88

Iago, 83

Immanuel ben Solomon, 9

Itinerarium Mentis in Deum, 94

Jason, 57

John, St., Apostle, 67

Jove, 5

Joyce, James, 66

Juan de la Cruz, San, 63

Justinian, 21, 35, 56, 59, 95

Kantorowicz, Ernst, 35

Latini, Brunetto, 23, 35, 52, 54, 55, 58, 69, 80, 82, 86, 88, 98

Lauretta, 53

Leah, 47

Leopardi, G., 6, 96

Lewis, C. S., 6

Lombardo, Marco, 56, 83, 94

Lucia, 101

Lucifer, 9, 26

Index

*

MacLeish, Archibald, 7
Manfred, 23, 32, 60
Manto, 56, 80
Mary, Virgin, 99
Matelda, 46–48
Matilda, Countess, 47
Mazzoni, Guido, 42
Mephistopheles, 98
Milton, 79, 81, 99
Minotaur, the, 40, 98
Minos, 38, 40, 41, 43
Momigliano, Attilio, 41
Montano, Rocco, 82
Moore, Edward, 71

Nibelungenlied, 89
Nicodemus, Gospel of, 36
Nimrod, 40
Novello, Federico, 22

Orso di Mangona, 22
Ovid, 9, 65
Orlando, 70
Owen, Sir, 11

Paul, St., Vision of, 9, 36
Peter, St., Apostle, 9, 32, 64;
    Apocalypse of, 8
Peter Damian, St., 23
Petrarch, 65, 72, 97, 98
Phlegyas, 41

Pia, 22, 52, 53, 57, 86
Piccarda, 21, 22, 57
Pier de la Brosse, 22
Pietro di Dante, 92
Plato, 65
Plutus, 40, 98
Posidonius, 36
Proust, Marcel, 66
Ptolemy, 36

Quasimodo, Salvatore, 63
Questio de Aqua et de
    Terra, 75–76

Rachel, 47
Roman de la Rose, 80
Rüegg, August, 11

Santayana, George, 4, 63
Sapegno, Natalino, 53
Sapia, 54, 56
Sartorises, the, 102
Satan, 26, 40, 98–100
Sayers, Dorothy, 12
Scala, Can Grande della, 97
Scaligeri, the, 72
Scartazzini, Giovanni, 47
Scott, Sir Walter, 92
Shakespeare, 3, 83
Sigier de Brabant, 57
Singleton, Charles, 47, 81

(114)

Sinon, 56, 75
Sisyphus, 8
Snopeses, the, 102
Sordello, 23, 25, 38, 46, 59
Spitzer, Leo, 31
Statius, 45, 56, 59, 66, 67, 76
Swing, T. K., 3

Tantalus, 8
Tasso, 79, 92
Thomas Aquinas, St., 21, 35, 59, 63, 65, 76
Tundale, 9, 10

Ugolino, 21, 38, 41, 56

Ulysses, 11, 18, 23, 51, 56, 80, 82, 99

Vico, Giambattista, 89, 103
Villani, Giovanni, 76, 84
Virgil, 4, 7, 9, 12, 18, 19, 25, 26, 28, 34, 36, 39–41, 47, 48, 56, 62, 63, 66–69, 79–81, 83, 87, 92, 93, 95
Visconti, Nino, 82, 83
Vita nuova, 12, 74, 75, 81
Vivaldi brothers, the, 11

Wilkins, E. H., 13
Williams, Charles, 63, 93

A selected list of MIDLAND BOOKS

MB-1	METAMORPHOSES *Ovid; tr. Humphries* (cl.$4.95s)	$1.95
MB-2	THE ART OF LOVE *Ovid; tr. Humphries*	$1.95
MB-6	THE DIPLOMACY OF THE AMERICAN REVOLUTION *Bemis*	$1.95
MB-7	THE LITERARY SYMBOL *Tindall*	$1.95
MB-12	THE DOUBLE *Dostoyevsky; tr. Bird*	$1.75
MB-14	AFRICAN NOTEBOOK *Schweitzer* (illus.)	$1.60
MB-15	THE MORAL DECISION: RIGHT AND WRONG IN THE LIGHT OF AMERICAN LAW *Cahn*	$2.25
MB-16	FORMS OF MODERN FICTION *O'Connor*	$1.75
MB-19	THE ESTHETIC BASIS OF GREEK ART *Carpenter* (illus.)	$1.75
MB-20	THE SATIRES OF JUVENAL *tr. Humphries* (cl. $5.00s)	$1.65
MB-24	AGE OF SURREALISM *Fowlie* (illus.)	$1.75
MB-25	COLERIDGE ON IMAGINATION *Richards*	$1.95
MB-26	JAMES JOYCE AND THE MAKING OF ULYSSES *Budgen* (illus.)	$2.25
MB-36	THE GOLDEN ASS *Apuleius; tr. Lindsay*	$1.85
MB-38	DANTE'S LA VITA NUOVA *tr. Musa*	$1.65
MB-40	THE DISCOVERY OF LANGUAGE: LINGUISTIC SCIENCE IN THE NINETEENTH CENTURY *Pedersen* (illus.) (cl. $6.50s)	$2.95
MB-42	AN INTRODUCTION TO THE GREEK THEATRE *Arnott* (illus.)	$2.45
MB-45	VERGIL'S AENEID *tr. Lind* (cl. $8.50s)	$1.95
MB-46	ESSAYS ON THE ODYSSEY: SELECTED MODERN CRITICISM *ed. Taylor* (cl. $6.00s)	$1.95
MB-47	THE LIVING THOUGHTS OF KIERKEGAARD *Auden*	$1.95
MB-51	ARIOSTO'S ORLANDO FURIOSO: SELECTIONS FROM SIR JOHN HARINGTON'S TRANSLATION *ed. Gottfried*	$2.95
MB-58	THE CHALLENGE OF EXISTENTIALISM *Wild*	$1.95
MB-65	EARLY MEDIEVAL ART *Kitzinger* (48 plates)	$1.95
MB-67	A STYLE MANUAL FOR STUDENTS *Seeber* (rev. ed.)	$1.00
MB-71	RATIONAL MAN: A MODERN INTERPRETATION OF ARISTOTELIAN ETHICS *Veatch*	$1.95
MB-73	BEOWULF *tr. Pearson; ed. Collins* (cl. $5.00s)	$1.65
MB-75	THE POPULATION CRISIS: IMPLICATIONS AND PLANS FOR ACTION *ed. Ng and Mudd*	$2.95
MB-76	A STYLE MANUAL FOR AUTHORS *Seeber*	$1.25
MB-77	THE WELL-TEMPERED CRITIC *Frye*	$1.75
MB-83	MYTH: A SYMPOSIUM *ed. Sebeok*	$2.45
MB-84	THE GOOD CITY *Haworth*	$1.75
MB-88	THE EDUCATED IMAGINATION *Frye* (cl. $4.50s)	$1.75
MB-89	FAULKNER: THE MAJOR YEARS: A CRITICAL STUDY *Backman* (cl. $6.75s)	$1.95
MB-90	THE WITHERING AWAY OF THE CITY *Willbern* (illus.)	$1.65
MB-91	TALES OF THE NORTH AMERICAN INDIANS *ed. Thompson* (cl. $7.50s)	$2.95
MB-97	THE PHENOMENOLOGY OF INTERNAL TIME-CONSCIOUSNESS *Husserl; ed. Heidegger; tr. Churchill* (cl. $6.50s)	$1.95
MB-99	THE DIPLOMACY OF A NEW AGE: MAJOR ISSUES IN U.S. POLICY SINCE 1945 *Perkins* (cl. $6.50s)	$2.45

(continued on next page)

MIDLAND BOOKS

MB-101 THE ODES OF HORACE: A CRITICAL STUDY *Commager* $2.95

MB-102 ENVIRONMENT FOR MAN: THE NEXT FIFTY YEARS *ed. Ewald* (cl. $6.95) $2.95

MB-104 FILM MAKERS ON FILM MAKING *ed. Geduld* (cloth $7.50s) $1.95

MB-108 THE TWICE-BORN: A STUDY OF A COMMUNITY OF HIGH-CASTE HINDUS *Carstairs* $2.65

MB-109 BOSSES IN LUSTY CHICAGO: THE STORY OF BATHHOUSE JOHN AND HINKY DINK *Wendt and Kogan* (cloth $6.95s) $2.95

MB-110 THE AMERICAN SCENE *James; ed. Edel* (cloth $10.00s) $3.95

MB-111 THE CONCEPT OF IRONY: WITH CONSTANT REFERENCE TO SOCRATES *Kierkegaard; tr. Capel* $2.95

MB-113 THE ART OF WILLIAM GOLDING *Oldsey and Weintraub* $1.95

MB-114 THE SHAKESPEAREAN IMAGINATION: A CRITICAL INTRODUCTION *Holland* $2.95

MB-115 MODERN GERMAN LITERATURE: THE MAJOR FIGURES IN CONTEXT *Hatfield* $1.85

MB-118 THE BURNING FOUNTAIN: A STUDY IN THE LANGUAGE OF SYMBOLISM (NEW AND REVISED EDITION) *Wheelwright* (cloth $8.50s) $2.95

MB-119 DICKENS AND CRIME *Collins* $2.95

MB-120 THE WIDENING GYRE: CRISIS AND MASTERY IN MODERN LITERATURE *Frank* $2.65

MB-121 FIVE PLAYS BY LANGSTON HUGHES; *ed. Smalley* (cloth $5.95s) $2.65

MB-122 METAPHOR AND REALITY *Wheelwright* (cloth $6.75s) $2.45

MB-123 THE PRESENT AGE IN BRITISH LITERATURE *Daiches* (cloth $8.50s) $2.65

MB-124 CHARLES DICKENS: THE WORLD OF HIS NOVELS *Miller* $2.95

MB-125 LUCRETIUS: THE WAY THINGS ARE: THE "DE RERUM NATURA" OF TITUS LUCRETIUS CARUS *tr. Humphries* (cloth $7.50) $1.95

MB-126 JAMES JOYCE TODAY: ESSAYS ON THE MAJOR WORKS *ed. Staley* (cloth $6.50s) $1.95

MB-127 SAINT JOAN OF THE STOCKYARDS *Brecht; tr. Jones* (cloth $5.45) $1.95

MB-128 SCIENCE AND INDUSTRY IN THE NINETEENTH CENTURY *Bernal* (cloth $6.50s) $2.95

MB-129 SHAKESPEARE AND THE RIVAL TRADITIONS *Harbage* $3.45

MB-130 THE WALL STREET LAWYER *Smigel* (cloth $8.50s) $2.95

MB-131 TENDER IS THE NIGHT: ESSAYS IN CRITICISM *ed. LaHood* (cloth $8.50s) $1.95

MB-132 ARISTOTLE AND THE AMERICAN INDIANS: A STUDY IN RACE PREJUDICE IN THE MODERN WORLD *Hanke* $1.95

MB-133 MANY THOUSAND GONE: THE EX-SLAVES' ACCOUNT OF THEIR BONDAGE AND FREEDOM *Nichols* $2.45

MB-134 FROM VERISMO TO EXPERIMENTALISM: ESSAYS ON THE MODERN ITALIAN NOVEL *ed. Pacifici* (cloth $7.50s) $2.95

MB-135 A MAN CALLED WHITE: THE AUTOBIOGRAPHY OF WALTER WHITE $3.25

MB-136 THE GIFT OF A COW: A TRANSLATION FROM THE HINDI NOVEL "GODAAN" *Premchand; tr. Roadarmel* (cloth $10.00s) $2.50

MB-137 TOUGH, SWEET AND STUFFY *Gibson* (cloth $4.50) $1.95

MB-138 PERSPECTIVES ON THE DIVINE COMEDY *Bergin* $1.65

MB-139 THE THEORY OF COMEDY *Olson* (cloth $4.50) $1.95

MB-140 THE PETTY DEMON *Sologub* $3.25